OUR LIVING TRADITION

OUR LIVING TRADITION

SEVEN CANADIANS

Edited by Claude T. Bissell

Published in association with

Carleton University by

University of Toronto Press

CONTENTS

INTRODUCTION

BY CLAUDE T. BISSELL

It is a common prejudice that it is neither wise nor profitable to print public addresses in book form. This is a prejudice that is particularly strong in Canada, possibly because, as a people, we subject ourselves to public addresses on a great variety of social occasions and have as a result developed a cynical immunity to the formal spoken word. The speech and the lecture, we believe, have ceremonial value, but they are not likely to survive the event that prompted them. And yet I think there need exist no cleavage between the spoken and the written forms of expression. One has only to look at the files of *The Listener* to realize that the spoken word can stand the closer scrutiny provided by the printed page. Like the good play, the speech or lecture, when turned into a book, often enjoys a second life. It becomes, indeed, an essay of a particularly attractive kind. At its best, it establishes an easy, direct relationship with the individual reader in the same way that it established an easy relationship with its original audience. It is distinguished by clarity and intelligibility, for, as first presented, its very success depended upon the existence of these qualities.

I think it can be said of all seven studies in this volume that they happily realize the potentialities of the public lecture and that, transferred to the printed page with only slight alterations, they retain the qualities of clarity, directness and liveliness that they possessed when given as public lectures at Carleton University. Here you will find not so much a series of formal expositions as a series of lively intellectual debates.

No attempt has been made to develop a common approach among the seven authors. Indeed, given the highly individual quality of the contributors, any such attempt would have amounted to an act of editorial folly. But the very nature of the subject-matter created, I think, a dominant theme. All of the men treated in this volume, whether they are statesmen, poets, novelists or journalists, possessed lively and vigorous minds, and they devoted much of their intellectual energy to what Frank Underhill has described as the great Canadian problem—the problem of our nationality. Like all basic problems, this one admits much banality and sentimentality, but none of the men treated in this volume were guilty of these sins against the spirit. They were all, in various ways, attached to the country in which they lived, and yet not one of them could be accused of non-critical patriotism. None of them was in any sense a little Canadian. They could rise above the local and national scenes and see problems in international perspective. Two of them indeed, Goldwin Smith and Frederick Philip Grove, came to this country with their minds formed by education and experiences in Europe. In one of them—Archibald Lampman—the comment on the national scene is always indirect. Never once in his poetry, as Munro Beattie points out, does Lampman use the words Canada or Canadian, but his best work is always a sensitive expression of a basic Canadian experience.

I would mention another unifying quality of these studies. It is this. There has been an attempt here to break down the traditional barrier between our politics and our literature. At the end of his paper, Malcolm Ross points out that "our living tradition is revealed to us not only in Hansard and in Royal Commission briefs, but also in the wars of the spirit." Too often our historians have seen Canadians simply as political and economic animals, and too often our literary critics have seen our writers simply as the exotic products of a thin literary culture. This is the reason, it seems to me, why frequently our history has seemed dull and lifeless, and our literature remote, rootless and unreal. All of the contributors to this volume have been able to do away with narrow specialist blinkers and to see their subjects not simply as full-time politicians or writers, but as interesting people. One cannot of course turn Edward Blake into a man of letters, or Lampman into a politician, or even Leacock into an economist. But, at least, one can take into consideration the fact that Lampman had lively and unorthodox views on political subjects, and that Blake, Macdonald and Laurier had literary interests and considerable gifts of expression. The sub-title of this volume, then, is accurate. These are seven Canadians, seven men of more than average intellectual ability and emotional sensitivity who lived and worked in this country and thought about its destiny.

The real unity of this volume, however, is simply a reflection of the contributors. All of the contributors are scholars, some of them indeed the authorities in their particular fields. Behind several of these essays stand works of major proportions. Mason Wade's study of Laurier has behind it his important work on the French-Canadians, and Donald Creighton's study of Sir John A. Macdonald is, as it were, a sprightly and pointed epilogue to his great biography. Frank Underhill is the authority both on Edward Blake and on the liberal tradition in Canadian politics of which Blake is a principal spokesman. All of these scholars, moreover, approach their subjects with enthusiasm and with a measure of sympathetic identification. Wilfrid Eggleston, for instance, knew Grove, and knows, too, the kind of experience in the Canadian West upon which Grove drew for his best work. These are not so much definitive distillations of scholarship as lively commentaries written by scholars. Throughout, I think, there has been a happy conjunction of author and subject, perhaps nowhere more happily than in the concluding study, where Robertson Davies, himself our most gifted writer in a humorous and satirical vein, examines incisively but always affectionately, the work of his great predecessor, Stephen Leacock.

CONTRIBUTORS

FRANK H. UNDERHILL is widely known as an historian and as a commentator on Canadian political life. He has recently published *The British Commonwealth: An Experiment in Co-operation among Nations*. He was formerly Professor of History at the University of Toronto, and is now Curator of Laurier House.

MALCOLM ROSS is the author of important studies of seventeenth-century English literature and is the editor of *Our Sense of Identity*, a collection of writings on Canadian themes. He is Professor of English and Dean of Arts at Trinity College in the University of Toronto.

DONALD G. CREIGHTON is the author of several major studies in Canadian history, and has written the definitive biography of Sir John A. Macdonald. He is Professor of History at the University of Toronto.

MUNRO BEATTIE is Chairman of the Department of English at Carleton University.

MASON WADE, author of *The French Canadians*, is Professor of History at the University of Western Ontario.

WILFRID EGGLESTON is a journalist with wide literary interests. He is the author of a study of the influence of the frontier in Canadian literature, *The Frontier in Canadian Letters*. He is Director of the Department of Journalism at Carleton University.

ROBERTSON DAVIES, novelist, dramatist, and critic, is Master of Massey College, Professor of English, and Edgar Stone Lecturer at the University of Toronto.

OUR LIVING TRADITION

EDWARD BLAKE

What makes an effective politician? During the summer of 1956 the B.B.C. ran a series of talks entitled "Letters to Beginners," "Letter to a Young Scientist," "Letter to a Young Painter," "Letter to a Young Musician," etc. Each so-called letter was written by an elder in the profession, and contained his advice to a young man beginning his career in the same field. Included in the series was a "Letter to a Young Politician," by Christopher Hollis, well-known writer on political themes and Conservative member of the British parliament.

> Don't go into politics [said Mr. Hollis] or at least do not stay there long if you are primarily a writer. . . . The practical politician must inevitably submit himself to a discipline of compromise—continuously say less than he would like to say in order to keep in step with his colleagues—be content with a sort of highest common factor of truth, because his purpose is to get something done. The writer must follow out the argument where it leads—deal his blows impartially to right and left—because his purpose is to say something. . . . Again, if you would go into parliament, you must be a little vulgar and more than a little vain. You cannot do this unless you like being noticed and standing on platforms and people cheering you. Vulgarity and vanity are not serious vices, but they are vices, and if you would be a politician, it is important to make sure that you have them. [*The Listener*, August 9, 1956.]

Edward Blake was not an effective politician. He was not a writer, like Mr. Hollis, but he *was* an intellectual and one of the

3

greatest lawyers of his time. He lacked vulgarity, and his vanity was that of the intellectual rather than of the politician. He was unable to bring himself continuously to say less than he would like to say in order to keep in step with his colleagues. As an intellectual and a lawyer, he was supremely good at critical analysis, and he strove to make his analysis comprehensive, clear and precise. But the lawyer who does well in politics must have an unlawyerlike genius for avoiding comprehension, clarity and precision. Blake enjoyed expounding a case, but he hated the necessity of those public performances in which the politician seeks the applause of the crowd. He was a painfully reserved and shy individual, with no capacity for playing the demagogue; and, lacking the demagogic flair, he lacked as well the thick hide which the politician needs in order to survive.

He was deficient also in another more vital quality which is a necessary equipment of the statesman in office: he had an abnormally small capacity for the exhilaration and inspiration that come from exercising power. He was always resigning. "To rule a people," exclaims Bertrand de Jouvenel, "what an extension of the ego is there!. . . that incomparable pleasure of radiating daily impulsions into an immense mass and prompting distant movements of millions of unknown limbs. It is not surprising that Colbert, coming to his desk in the morning, rubbed his hands for joy." (*On Power*, New York, 1949, p. 121.) Blake never rubbed his hands for joy, unless perhaps after a good day in court. Macdonald and Laurier and King must have rubbed their hands for joy every morning as they walked into the prime minister's office in the East Block.

So Edward Blake was a failure in politics. He was the most tragic failure that has yet appeared in our Canadian public life. Yet he started the great game of politics with an incomparable advantage. He was born in a log cabin. The most astounding feature of Blake's career is that he hardly ever referred to this fact, which should have been worth thousands of votes at every election. The man was obviously not cut out for North American politics.

Edward Blake was born on October 13, 1833, on a pioneer farm in the backwoods of southwestern Upper Canada, near the present town of Strathroy. He died in Toronto on March 1, 1912. He was a member of the Canadian parliament from 1867 to 1892; a member of the Ontario legislature from 1867 to 1872, and premier of Ontario for part of a year, 1871–1872. He was a cabinet minister in the Alexander Mackenzie administration of the 1870's, the first liberal government of Canada after Confederation, and Minister of Justice from 1875 to 1877. He led the Liberal opposition in Ottawa from 1880 to 1887. After retiring from Canadian politics in 1892, he was an Irish Nationalist member of the British parliament from 1892 to 1907, and a member of the inner executive of the Irish Nationalist group during those years. He was also Chancellor of the University of Toronto, his Alma Mater, from 1873 to 1900. Finally, he was the leading lawyer of his day in Canada, and four times declined high judicial office: once in 1869 when Sir John Macdonald would have made him head of the Chancery Court in Ontario— the position which his father had held; once in 1875 when Alexander Mackenzie offered him the first Chief Justiceship of the newly established Supreme Court of Canada (a Chief Justice at the age of forty-one!) ; once in 1896 when Sir Wilfrid Laurier offered him his choice of the Chief Justiceship of the Supreme Court or of the Ontario Appeal Court; and once in 1905 when Laurier again offered him the Supreme Court, and then tried to get him appointed to the Judicial Committee of the Privy Council.

Blake's family came from Ireland. The original Blakes were Catholic gentry in Galway in the southwest, where they had been settled since the twelfth century. After the great Catholic defeat in the seventeenth century one branch of the family had turned Protestant. And at the end of the eighteenth century a Dominick Blake appears, a graduate of Trinity College, Dublin, and a parson in the Church of Ireland. He married a daughter of William Hume, who was an Anglo-Irish squire, the owner of the estate of Humewood in County Wicklow some forty miles south of Dublin. The Rev. Dominick Blake died in 1823 leaving a widow with a family; and in 1832 she decided to emigrate with her family to Upper Canada. By this time her eldest son, also named Dominick, had followed his father into the Church of

Ireland. Her second son, William Hume Blake, had gone through Trinity College, started to train for a medical career, but abandoned this, had some thoughts of entering the church, and then in 1832, a young man without many prospects, had married a cousin in the Hume family. Dominick and William Hume with their wives accompanied their mother and their sisters to Canada. Arriving in Toronto in the summer of 1832, Dominick was sent by Archdeacon Strachan to a parish in Adelaide township away in the backwoods just then being opened for settlement west of London. William Hume abandoned whatever aspirations he may have had for the church; and having thus given up two careers without persisting in either, decided to become a pioneer farmer, apparently in the hope of building up a landed estate in the tradition of his Blake and Hume ancestors back in Ireland. He took up a holding near where his clerical brother was located. Here next fall his first child was born, a boy, and christened Dominick Edward Blake. Apparently the father and mother decided shortly after this that they were not fitted for pioneer farming; and in the next year, 1834, they moved back to Toronto, where William Hume Blake, having now abandoned three possible careers, plunged into law.

His success in this profession was remarkable. Once admitted to the bar of Upper Canada, after a few years' hard work as a student in a Toronto law office, he soon made himself one of the leading barristers of the province. Whether because the Humes had been Whigs back in Ireland or because living in Toronto just naturally drove a man of sensitive intelligence towards the left in politics—it still does—William Hume Blake espoused the Reform Cause, supported his friend Robert Baldwin, and became Solicitor-General West in the great LaFontaine-Baldwin administration of the late 1840's. He took a prominent part in the exciting debates over the Rebellion Losses bill, was challenged to a duel by a young Tory named John A. Macdonald, and saw the burning of the parliament buildings in Montreal in the riots of 1849. At this moment he cut short his political career, when Baldwin induced him to become head of the Chancery Court in Upper Canada.

William Hume Blake's children therefore grew up not on a

pioneer farm but in one of the leading professional families in Toronto. Edward Blake—he early stopped using the Dominick in his name—and his younger brother, Samuel, after having private tutors at home, attended Upper Canada College and then the University of Toronto, and followed their father into the legal profession. Edward was head boy at Upper Canada, and graduated from University with the silver medal in classics: he was among the *élite* as a student.

Edward Blake had the same quick success as a lawyer that his father had had. By 1867 he was the senior partner in what was already one of the leading legal firms in Toronto. He had also been marked out as promising political material. At the great Upper Canadian Reform convention, called in June 1867 to draw up a platform for the Grit party in the new federal Canada, he was chosen by George Brown to move the first resolution. He ran as a Grit candidate in both the federal and the provincial elections—and was successful in both contests.

In Ontario in 1867 the Grits suffered a setback which they had not expected, with the result that John A. Macdonald became first prime minister of Canada at the head of a professedly coalition cabinet, and John Sandfield Macdonald became first premier of Ontario at the head of a similar coalition cabinet. The Grits in opposition in Toronto, after a period of fumbling, chose young Edward Blake to be their leader. And in 1871, as the result of the second provincial election, Blake ousted Sandfield Macdonald and became the first Liberal premier of Ontario, with Alexander Mackenzie of Sarnia as his chief lieutenant in the post of provincial treasurer. He did not, however, hold this office for long. In 1872 legislation was passed forbidding dual representation; and Blake and Mackenzie both opted for the federal sphere. Blake persuaded his friend and fellow lawyer, Oliver Mowat, who had been one of George Brown's lieutenants at the Quebec conference in 1864 but had then gone on to the bench, to return to politics and take his position as premier of Ontario. For the next twenty years Blake in Ottawa and Mowat in Toronto operated as political and legal allies in fighting against the Macdonald system for what they conceived to be the proper liberal conception of the Canadian federal union. They usually beat Macdonald in the courts on the interpretation of the British North America Act, but they were not able to oust him from political power in Ottawa.

There was, of course, one short interval of Liberal political success at Ottawa in these years. During the first sessions of parliament after 1867 the Ontario Grits, the Rouge group from Quebec and the sprinkling of opposition members from the Maritimes gradually formed themselves into a united opposition under the leadership of Alexander Mackenzie. Mackenzie was now the senior Grit in public life, since George Brown had retired. A good many of his colleagues would have preferred the younger and more gifted Edward Blake as leader of the party. But Blake, busy with a heavy legal practice, was also leading the provincial party in Toronto, and he refused to be considered as a possible federal leader. The result was that, when the Liberals unearthed the Pacific Scandal in 1873 and drove Macdonald from office, it was Mackenzie who became prime minister.

Unfortunately for themselves the Liberals came into power just when the great depression of 1873 was spreading over the world. After five depression years of office, without being able to accomplish anything of great note, they were defeated in 1878. They had a respectable programme of legislation to their credit; but they had not got the Pacific railway going, and they had allowed Macdonald to seize upon the new attractive cry of the so-called National Policy. They seemed to lack, or could easily be made by opposition critics to seem to lack, the dynamic adventurous qualities which marked the Conservative party under Macdonald. And when Blake took over the leadership from Mackenzie in 1880, the party still seemed to be critical and pessimistic rather than constructive and optimistic about Canada's destiny. Blake was therefore unable to make headway against the magic appeal of John A. After being defeated in the general elections of 1882 and 1887, he retired from the leadership, despairing of his own ability to win popular support. It was left to Laurier to produce gradually a Liberal party which could effectively challenge the Conservatives as the nation-building party of Canada; though Laurier, as I shall show, carried to fruition after 1896 some of the policies to which Blake had unsuccessfully tried to convert his party in the 1880's.

II

What was liberalism in the Canada of this generation from the 1860's to the 1890's? Until recently we had become so accustomed to the phenomenon of government by a Liberal party (Liberal with a capital "L") that we tended to accept it, at least in Ottawa, as the result of natural law. Inevitably in such circumstances the Liberal party in office ceased to be a party of distinctive ideas or ideals. It was the party of administration, efficient and practical as a good administrator should be, but also unimaginative, complacent, authoritarian, slightly cynical, as all successful people who sit too long in offices tend to become, living as they do in a present which will never be succeeded by a future and whose past is embalmed in the office files.

Moreover the political government and the non-political civil service have become so merged together in office over the years, that one needs to have lived longer in Ottawa than I have to be able to distinguish them at all clearly. For the inarticulate major premise of the civilization of Ottawa, as one sensed it coming from outside, was that, whatever the question at issue at any moment might be, there sat somewhere in some Ottawa office a personage, benevolent, omniscient, omnipotent, who knew on that particular issue what was good for people better than they could conceivably know themselves. In short, it has been almost impossible to be a liberal with a small "l" in the Ottawa of the 1950's.

How explain, then, a man like Edward Blake, who was always a somewhat uneasy party man, who was never very happy in administering or manipulating other people, who indeed during his whole career held public administrative office for only three or four years, and who, in the most famous of all his utterances, the Aurora speech of 1874, declared that he would rather be a private in the advanced guard of liberalism than an officer in the main body?

When Edward Blake entered public life the term Liberal was just emerging in Canadian political phraseology as an alternative to the old term Reform or Reformer. Blake and some of his friends soon became restless under the intellectual dictatorship of George Brown and the *Globe*. By the middle seventies, con-

9

sidering themselves as a left wing in the Reform party, they were apt to refer to themselves as Liberals in distinction from the old-time Grits, the followers of Brown, the devout readers of the *Globe*, the partisan supporters of the Alexander Mackenzie administration. In 1875 they launched a new daily paper in Toronto, the *Liberal*, which they hoped would break up the *Globe*'s domination over Reform journalism in Ontario. The failure of the *Liberal* after a few months was in itself a sign of the weakness of the left wing and of the strength of the Brownites. And as a matter of fact most people came to use the words Reform, Liberal, and Grit indiscriminately for the party—Grit remaining as the popular nickname, and Liberal gradually replacing Reform as the official name during the decade of the 1880's.

There were some critics who denied that Canadian party divisions had any meaning at all in post-Confederation conditions. "But in this country, now that responsible and Parliamentary government has been finally conceded, the franchise extended almost as far as anybody wishes to extend it, and religious equality established by the secularization of the Clergy Reserves, what is there for a Conservative to conserve or a Reformer to reform?" So wrote the newly arrived Oxford professor and Manchester Liberal, Goldwin Smith, in April 1872 in one of his first Bystander articles in the *Canadian Monthly*. This was also the thesis of the "Canada First" movement which launched itself before the public in 1874 by the founding of the National Club in Toronto, the issuing of a manifesto, and the starting of a new monthly journal, *The Nation*. "Canada First" called on Canadians to emancipate themselves from the old feuds and jealousies of the days before 1867 and to start the new era with an invigorating devotion to the new nationality—Canada First as against the old sectional and provincial loyalties, Canada First as against the old Macdonald-Brown strife, Canada First as against the old colonial subordination to Britain. Both Goldwin Smith and "Canada First" looked to Edward Blake, that uneasy Grit, as the possible leader of a new political movement.

This first decade of Confederation teemed with discussion of the implications—political, economic and cultural—of the new

Canadian nationality. In fact, it is impossible to read the discussion of these years without coming to the conclusion that nothing new on the subject has been said since. Studying the development of our Canadian nationality since 1867, one comes to feel more and more like a squirrel running forever inside a revolving cage and never getting anywhere. As Sir John Willison once remarked: "With every change of government in Canada we are made into a nation over again."

Edward Blake, beginning his career in the midst of the first fine careless rapture of Canadian nationalism, found this kind of discussion very congenial during most of his life. He did not accept the thesis of the *Globe* that Canadians should now settle down and work their new institutions for a generation instead of always tinkering with them and asking themselves questions about them. He had resigned from the Mackenzie government early in 1874, after a few weeks in office; and it was as a private member of parliament, and already a somewhat troublesome one, that on October 3 he went up to a Liberal demonstration at Aurora and there delivered a disturbing speech which supplied subject-matter for editorials in Canadian papers for weeks.

In the Aurora speech Blake was clearly trying to set out his conception of what Liberalism meant or should mean in the 1870's. He wasted little time praising the achievements of the Liberal governments then in office in Ottawa and Toronto. The fundamental need of the country, he told his audience, was the development of a national spirit.

We are engaged in a very difficult task—the task of welding together seven provinces which have been accustomed to regard themselves as isolated from each other. . . . How are we to effect a real union between these provinces? Can we do it by giving a sop now to one, now to another, in the manner of the late government? Not so! . . . We must find some other and truer ground on which to unite, some common aspiration to be shared, and I think it can be found alone in the cultivation of that national spirit to which I have referred.

Canada must therefore, he thought, take the responsibility for her own foreign policy; otherwise "we are four millions of Britons who are not free." The best way he saw of doing this at the time

11

was through an imperial federation in which Canada would cease to be a dependent colony and would become an equal partner with Britain.

He condemned the extravagant commitment of the late Macdonald government to build a transcontinental railway to British Columbia within ten years. If the Columbians really demanded secession because of the delays in building the railway, he would let them go. He went on to other more academic topics, such as Senate reform—though, of course, in 1874 nobody yet knew that this was an academic topic—proportional representation, the ballot, extension of the franchise, and compulsory voting. And he ended by quoting at length from his favourite poet, Alfred Tennyson: "You ask me, why, tho' ill at ease, Within this region I subsist," leading up to his conclusion that Canada was, or should be, a land where freedom broadened slowly down from precedent to precedent.

The Aurora speech caused more public argument than any other utterance by a Canadian politician in that generation. Blake published its text in a pamphlet, entitled *A National Sentiment*, along with editorials in newspapers and journals about it; and this pamphlet still makes very interesting reading. Critics pointed out that if a national sentiment was his aim, imperial federation was a strange way to seek it, since close constitutional union with Britain would surely produce, if successful, an imperial British sentiment. After the country went in for economic nationalism with the National Policy tariff, Blake himself reached the conclusion that, as he put it, the train had gone past the imperial federation station; and he reverted to the ideal which has always been most congenial to Canadian Liberals, that of an independent, but not separatist, national sovereignty.

The other ideas in the Aurora speech, apart from his scepticism about the rate of Canada's continental expansion, stirred little lasting interest. As several commentators remarked, there was no proposal in the speech which would contribute to the material development of the country. That was it. Material development. The man who was to make the really effective appeal to the incipient national sentiment was not Blake but John A. Macdonald; the Macdonald tariff and railway policies were to canalize Canadian national aspirations along economic lines rather than along the political lines that interested Blake—and also, incidentally, along American lines. For Macdonald, with his close alliance between the national government and big business corporations, was the chief Americanizing influence in Canadian politics during this first generation after 1867.

There was undoubtedly more than a little in the Aurora speech that might have justified the same sneering comment on Blake that Disraeli had made a short time previously when he first saw John Stuart Mill sitting in the House of Commons: "Ah, the political finishing governess." Blake had evidently been reading Mill, as his remarks on nationalism and on proportional representation showed.

It is perhaps worth noting here that nearly all the Canadian Liberals who were now in the 1870's rising to positions of leadership showed this same tendency to look to Britain for models of political thought and action rather than to the United States—in contrast to earlier radicals like Mackenzie, Papineau and the original Grits. In 1877 Laurier, in his famous Quebec speech on Political Liberalism, held up the English Whigs as his models; he repudiated the secular anti-clericalism of the European continent, and never mentioned the Liberty, Equality and Fraternity of the France of 1789 or the Jeffersonian and Jacksonian ideas which had attracted earlier members of his own Rouge group.

Blake and Mowat, Laurier's Ontario allies, were in their temperament, their legal training and their favourite reading, English Liberal Whigs rather than North American radical democrats. They were on the popular side, but didn't quite consider themselves as belonging to the populace. When Blake had recourse to poetry it was the English Tennyson whom he quoted, not the American Walt Whitman. Blake and Mackenzie did have one North American attribute in common. They did not bask in the smiles of English Society (with a capital S) as did John A. Macdonald; they were uncomfortable in the midst of English class divisions and what they felt was the snobbery of the English governing class; they both refused titles in 1877— though on the subject of titles, Canadian Liberals were not all of one mind. But the important point is that none of these men looked to Washington or New York or Boston for inspiration;

much less did they look to those parts of the United States where Granger and Populist storms were beginning to blow up.

III

One immediate effect of the Aurora speech was that a group of leading Liberals in parliament became alarmed at the danger of cleavage within the party and took steps to bring Blake and Mackenzie together again. In May 1875 Blake re-entered the cabinet as Minister of Justice. I should like now to go on to deal briefly with his views on Canadian national autonomy, on trade and tariff questions, on westward expansion and on English-French relations within Canada.

During the Mackenzie régime Blake was the chief thorn in the side of the Governor-General, Lord Dufferin. As a British liberal, Dufferin believed that Britain would have to yield continuously to Canadian pressure for the expansion of the range of self-government. But he always felt that Blake was pressing too hard, and that Blake had a bad influence on Mackenzie. Lord Carnarvon, the Colonial Secretary, shared these feelings. The chief subject on which these two Imperial officials and the Canadian Liberal government clashed was that of the dispute between the federal government and British Columbia over the delays in building the Pacific railway. I shall pause a while over one incident in this long controversy because it illustrates so well the differences between the Imperial authorities, who were worried lest the new Dominion should break up, and the Canadian government, who considered this a purely domestic dispute with which Downing St. was not concerned.

Lord Carnarvon had already intervened once in this quarrel, in 1874, when he induced the disputants to accept his mediation and handed down the so-called Carnarvon Terms, the chief item in which was that Canada, in compensation for delays in the main line, should build an extra local line on Vancouver Island from Nanaimo to Esquimalt. When Mackenzie introduced the necessary legislation to provide for the Esquimalt line, Blake, at that moment a private member, voted against it; and the bill was thrown out in the Senate. British Columbia refused a money equivalent for the Esquimalt line. The quarrel dragged on, and in 1876 Dufferin got the idea of trying to settle it by taking a trip to the coast himself and using his Irish blarney upon the Pacific politicians in the hope that he could get an agreement where his stiff-necked Grit government had failed. His advisers reluctantly let him go, warning him that his trip could only be in the nature of a gubernatorial progress and not at all a mission to conduct political negotiations. He came back with what he thought a brilliant solution. Let Lord Carnarvon once again mediate, but with a private understanding between the Colonial Secretary and the Governor-General that he would give a decision satisfactory to Ottawa and would thus use his Imperial authority to quiet down the windy Pacific politicians until the railway surveys should be complete and steps be taken to find private entrepreneurs to build the transcontinental line.

But Mackenzie had had enough of Imperial intervention by this time and flatly vetoed Dufferin's scheme. The discussion between the Governor and his advisers went on all that autumn, and came to a climax in two stormy interviews at Rideau Hall on November 16 and 18, 1876. I am going to read Mackenzie's account of these interviews, which he wrote out in a memorandum immediately after they took place. Dufferin also wrote an account of them in a private letter to Carnarvon. The two accounts show that this must have been one of the moments of greatest strain between the Canadian and British authorities in all the period since Responsible Government had been inaugurated. The two accounts don't quite agree at every point. Dufferin's letter gives the impression that the Governor was not the only one who lost control of himself. He says that "Mackenzie's aspect was simply pitiable, and Blake was upon the point of crying, as he very readily does when he is excited."

At any rate, here is Mackenzie's account. (The original is in the Alexander Mackenzie Letter Books in the Public Archives of Canada. It is reprinted in C. W. de Kiewiet and F. H. Underhill, *Dufferin-Carnarvon Correspondence, 1874–1878* (Champlain Society, 1955), p. 406. Dufferin's letter to Carnarvon is on page 309 of this volume.)

On the 16th I visited Rideau Hall. . . . I at once informed Lord Dufferin that I had consulted my colleagues and we were agreed that there was nothing more to be done on our part. . . . The

15

Government had determined to proceed with the construction of the Railway as fast as the resources of the country will permit. . . . Lord Dufferin then asked me in an excited manner if I meant to tell him that the language of our Minute of Council of September 1875 was definite and clear. . . . I said I certainly thought so. He then said it was not so, that Blake had prepared a trap for these people to walk into . . . and that he (Lord D) considered that Minute and the March one disgraceful.

I then told him that the Minute was written mainly by me. . . . Lord D then complained that I had taken in Mr. Mills, a declared enemy of Columbia, having already Mr. Blake and Mr. Cartwright both hostile. I replied that all three men were entirely agreed with myself as to what our course should be and what it had been since Mr. Blake entered into the government. Lord D then said we were not using Lord Carnarvon well, and that he (Lord D) felt his own honour involved. I replied to his angry remark that Lord Carnarvon should not have pressed his interference upon us, that I always regretted even the partial reference to him; that in a great country like this it was not well for Colonial Secretaries to be too ready in interfering with questions having no bearing on Imperial interests. I further remarked that I was unable to see how his (Lord D's) honour had been touched, that we were responsible for the acts of the government not him, that he had nothing to do with it except as a constitutional governor, and that we had to be responsible to the people of Canada and no one else. . . .

On the morning of the 18th I received a letter from Lord Dufferin in which he remarked that he "had not felt at all satisfied with our interview." . . . On the afternoon Mr. Blake and I had an interview of two and a half hours. . . .

(I omit Mackenzie's account of about the first half of this interview.)

A long and painful discussion ensued on the construction and meaning of Minutes of Council. . . . His Excellency was pleased to characterize [certain] passages . . . in very strong terms. He said they were deceitful and most disgraceful, and that if he had understood them he would have refused his assent and protected Lord Carnarvon from occupying false ground. . . .

After a lengthy discussion chiefly with Mr. Blake in which His Excellency reverted over and over again to the same topics, he turned to me and in a very excited tone said: "I call upon you to answer this question. I have a right to call upon you as Prime Minister to answer me now, and I insist upon an answer. I call upon you to tell me distinctly what you meant by 'compensation for delays' in your Minute referring to the Island railway."

I replied that I had no objection to answer any question properly put, but that he had no right in a verbal discussion to demand an answer in such a manner. . . . His Lordship after this scene spoke more calmly, and I embraced the opportunity to tell him that Lord Carnarvon and he must remember that Canada was not a Crown Colony (or a Colony at all in the ordinary acceptation of the term), that 4,000,000 of people, with a government responsible to the people only, could not and would not be dealt with as small communities had sometimes been dealt with; that we were capable of managing our own affairs, and the country would insist on doing it, and that no government could survive who could attempt, even at the insistence of a Colonial Secretary, to trifle with Parliamentary decisions.

His Lordship said he admitted that. In a few minutes he asked me if we took the ground that the construction of the Island railway, or the substituted money payment, was a general compensation. I said it was. He at once sprang to his feet and in a very violent tone said: "Well after that there is no use having any further discussion. I feel ashamed of it." Mr. Blake and I at once took our hats and moved towards the door, when he stopped me and said: "Don't let us quarrel about it. Sit down again and let us discuss it quietly, and don't mind what has happened." We accordingly sat down, but nothing further of any moment occurred, and very soon he said it was probably useless to discuss the matter further then. To this we assented. He then shook hands with both and said to me: "I hope, Mackenzie, you won't mind what has happened tonight. I was too hasty but meant no ill." . . . I replied: "It is all between ourselves," and the interview terminated.

And so it remained all between themselves and Lord Carnarvon. No hint of the differences between Dufferin and Carnarvon on one side and the Mackenzie government on the other was given to the public; and to this day only the historically learned part of the public has come to know of the stormy interviews in Rideau Hall in mid-November, 1876.

Perhaps it should be added, as another proof that the strain between the Canadian and the British governments never becomes quite unbearable, that after tempers on both sides cooled down, a few months later, in 1877, Lord Carnarvon offered knighthoods to Mackenzie and Blake. Dufferin and Mackenzie continued to correspond in a friendly fashion long after Dufferin had left Canada. And in 1883, when Carnarvon did a tour in Canada, he stayed while in Toronto in the home of Edward Blake, and put some of his money into Canadian investments on Blake's advice.

This determination, however, of Mackenzie and Blake that the effective decisions about Canada should be made by responsible Canadians, and not by anybody else, showed itself frequently during the Mackenzie régime. It is in fact the chief mark of this first Liberal government after Confederation.

In 1875 parliament passed the Act creating the Supreme Court of Canada. The Act contained a clause (Clause 47) purporting to abolish any appeals to British courts; and the Imperial government took objection to this clause—as did Macdonald and the Canadian Conservatives. In the summer of 1876 Blake, as Minister of Justice, went over to London to discuss this issue directly with Lord Carnarvon and Lord Cairns, the Lord Chancellor in the Disraeli government. He fretted and fumed through most of July and August, obtaining very infrequent interviews with his "lords and masters," as he called them in a letter to Mackenzie. Eventually the British government allowed the Supreme Court Act to stand, Blake being forced to agree that Clause 47 was inoperative because of its peculiar wording. But when he tried to get a promise from Downing St. that, if he introduced another amending clause which would effectively bar the appeal, it would not be disallowed, he was completely unsuccessful.

Blake presented all the arguments against the appeal to the Privy Council with which we have become familiar today: that, if Canadian legislators were competent to pass laws for Canada, Canadian judges should be competent to interpret them; that the appeal was very costly, involved long delays in justice, and was abused by rich litigants at the expense of poor ones: that the appeal to the foot of the throne, so-called, was purely mythical —in fact it was an appeal from Canadian to English judges, and Canadian judges were just as much Her Majesty's judges as were English ones—the metaphorical foot of the throne, that is, could be located in Ottawa as well as in London; that it was insulting to suggest that Canadian judges could not be impartial; and that, because of their experience of living in a federally organized community, they were in some ways better fitted to interpret a federal constitution than English judges could be. But the appeal remained until our own day.

Must there not have been some serious weakness in the intellectual fabric of Canadian liberalism in that it was not until the age of St. Laurent that Canadian Liberals once again reached, on the subject of judicial appeals, the position taken up by Blake and Mackenzie in the 1870's? Or is it significant that later in his life Blake changed his mind, and came to regard the appeal as a useful part of the Canadian federal system?

On trade questions generally, Blake decided to try to re-orient the policy of his party when he became responsible for it. The Mackenzie government had gone down to defeat in 1878 flying the Cobdenite flag to the last; and Blake had accepted his party's stand, though he devoted little personal attention to trade questions. But after Macdonald's National Policy tariff was established, Blake reached the conclusion that a country like Canada, committed to a costly policy of expansion, must incur, and had in fact already incurred such a volume of public expenditure, that some kind of a tariff high enough to be protectionist was necessary if the government was to balance its budget. It was unrealistic, therefore, if not dishonest, for the Liberals to hold out any hope (or threat) of far-reaching tariff reductions. In both the 1882 and the 1887 elections Blake announced that, if elected, his party would make reductions in particular items of the tariff schedules, but that protected manufacturers could look for a general continuity in tariff policy. Unfortunately this sensible policy did not go far enough to convince the manufacturers that it was worth while to abandon their support of Macdonald, while it alarmed the free-trade wing of Blake's own party. A strong group under Cartwright continued to make Cobdenite speeches which were clearly at variance with the speeches of the party leader. But the point to note here is that Blake already in the early 1880's was trying to make the shift in Liberal tariff policy which the Laurier-Fielding tariff eventually accomplished in 1897.

At this same time some of Blake's followers were pressing him to take another step in the opposite direction, to which he was decidedly opposed. Large sections of the Canadian public, especially among the farmers, still dreamt of Reciprocity with the United States and the free entry of Canadian natural products into the American market which had been enjoyed under the Treaty of 1854. But when George Brown in 1874 had tried to get a renewal of the Reciprocity Treaty the Americans had made it perfectly clear that Reciprocity had no interest for them unless it included the free entry of American manufactured goods into Canada. Should Canada consider an unrestricted reciprocity of this kind? This was the proposition put up to Blake by some of his followers. He rejected it because he feared that economic ties with the United States which were too close and too exclusive would be dangerous to Canadian political independence. After Blake retired in 1887 from the party leadership, however, Laurier was persuaded by Cartwright to take up the programme of Unrestricted Reciprocity as the chief Liberal policy. He badly burnt his fingers in this experiment; for Macdonald in the exciting election of 1891 succeeded in smearing the Liberals with the charge of disloyalty. "A British subject I was born, a British subject I will die." Macdonald, in fact, seized upon the political implications of this economic policy, which was exactly the point that Blake had emphasized in private to his followers before 1887.

Blake disagreed with the Laurier policy in 1891. Since, as ex-leader of the party, he could hardly run in his constituency of West Durham without expressing his views publicly, he retired from Canadian politics altogether. He did not want to retire, but neither did he want to injure Laurier in the election. So he drafted a long letter to his West Durham constituents explaining his objections to Unrestricted Reciprocity, a letter which Laurier persuaded him not to publish till after the election. When the letter came out on the very next day after the election, it produced an explosion and made a break between Blake and his party from which he never quite recovered.

Blake and Laurier did renew friendly relations. In the early months of 1892 the two of them were busy trying to work out an agreed statement on trade policy. Their efforts failed for the moment since Laurier, as a practical politician, was unwilling to admit publicly that he had been wrong in 1891. Whereupon Blake threw up the whole business and accepted an invitation from the Irish Nationalist party to join them in the struggle for Home Rule in the British parliament. He didn't mean this to be his final farewell to Canadian politics, but that is what it turned out to be.

Next year, 1893, at the Liberal convention in Ottawa, Blake's old party quietly ditched Unrestricted Reciprocity and went back to a moderate tariff policy which was, in effect, just what Blake had advocated all through the 1880's. But it was Laurier after 1896, in spite of his aberration in 1891, who was to reap all the political benefits of this policy of Blake's.

It has remained a puzzle to many that a man like Blake, so determined upon Canadian political autonomy, vis à vis both Britain and the United States, should have seemed, during his days of party leadership, so unimaginative in economic matters, so negative and critical towards all policies of economic expansion, and especially towards the great project of the Canadian Pacific Railway. Blake's career, it must be remembered, was passed mainly in the days of economic depression. His constant fear was lest Canada ruin her future economic possibilities by overstraining her present financial capacities. In the seventies he and all other Liberals regarded the Pacific railway scheme, as embodied in Macdonald's optimistic promises to British Columbia, as almost insane. Blake remained critical throughout the eighties. His railway policy would have been to build the line gradually, starting with the prairie section which would attract population, and advancing step by step thereafter as the country's population grew. This was very like the policy being pursued by James J. Hill, the empire-builder south of the border, in the construction of his Great Northern line from St. Paul to the Pacific.

Blake hammered away session after session about undue costs and over-rosy calculations. He denounced the C.P.R. monopoly in the West. He drew attention to the unhealthy relationship which was being built up between a government and a government party on one side and a monopolistic railway corporation on the other. He and his lieutenants attacked the corruption that ensued when speculators rushed to reap juicy profits from land grants and other concessions in the West.

But what could the Liberals in opposition do about it? For in Canada as well as in the United States this was the age of "The Great Barbecue." And Liberalism had no practicable alternative to the great barbecue as a method of achieving material expansion. The servings from the great barbecue to the lucky ones be-

21

came even more lavish, as a matter of fact, under Laurier than they had been under Macdonald. What *can* liberalism mean in a society such as this of business men on the make?

There was another field in which Blake tried to educate his party to a broader understanding of liberal principles. He was always proud of the fact that his father had been a member of the LaFontaine-Baldwin administration, the first party government in Canadian history in which English- and French-Canadians had worked together. But under George Brown the Upper Canada Grits had drifted away from this liberal tradition. Brown's anti-Catholic and anti-French fervour made it difficult for any French-Canadians to work with the Grits. And their natural allies in Quebec, the Rouge group, found themselves in their own local community facing a bitterly hostile Church. The ferocious ultra-montane campaign in Quebec in the 1870's against liberalism of any description made it almost impossible for a party calling itself Liberal to survive. Laurier's speech of 1877 on Political Liberalism, in which he enunciated the right of Catholic laymen to vote liberal if they wished, regardless of clerical direction, in which he warned of the danger of a purely French Catholic party, but in which at the same time he repudiated the extreme anti-clericalism of the early Rouge leaders, was an attempt to lay the basis of an effective Liberal party in Quebec; but it took Laurier nearly twenty years before he succeeded.

In the federal sphere in the 1880's Blake and Laurier, trying to present a Liberalism that would mean the same thing in Quebec and in Ontario, were thwarted by the explosion of racial and religious passion over the Riel affair in 1885. The English Protestant fanaticism of Ontario confronted the French Catholic fanaticism of Quebec. When Blake and Laurier in parliament attacked the hanging of Riel, a large part of Blake's Ontario followers deserted him. And when the federal election came in 1887 the Liberals were defeated. In despair Blake threw up the party leadership, because he had failed to overcome this English-French antipathy and to educate his own English-Canadian followers into a greater tolerance. But here again, Laurier was to reap where Blake had sown. In the long run it was Blake's constant attention to the Quebec point of view, his constant effort to educate the English part of his party, that helped Laurier in *his* greatest achievement, the building up of an effective bi-racial Liberal party in Canada.

All this time, Blake in Ottawa, with Laurier's assistance, and Mowat in Toronto had been fighting Macdonald on another issue closely connected with that of English-French relations, that of provincial rights. It is not possible here to go into the particular incidents of their long political and legal battle in this field. Let me say only that Macdonald did great harm to his country by his persistent endeavours to fit the new nationality into a rigid centralist framework. Blake and Mowat stood for that looser form of federal union which all our experience has shown to be the only degree of unity that we Canadians are likely to find tolerable. We are a deeply pluralistic community. At the same time it should be said that the Blake-Mowat provincial-rights doctrine was a flexible, pragmatic, this-worldly concept; it was provincial rights before the concept had been inflated into its present pathological state of exaggeration by the high-flying Hegelian metaphysics of Lord Haldane and the dogmatic, self-righteous fundamentalist theology of M. Duplessis and his French nationalist lawyers.

IV

It will be evident to the reader by this time that the man who was coming to play a bigger and bigger part in Edward Blake's career was Wilfrid Laurier. I should like to end my lecture by spending a little time upon the personal relations of these two great liberals. And perhaps I may here interpolate two political stories which I first heard a good many years ago from the late J. W. Dafoe, the editor of the *Winnipeg Free Press*. One story is about Laurier and the other about Blake.

Dafoe grew up in eastern Ontario in a Conservative family, and early went into journalism, working for the Montreal *Star*. In 1884 he was sent to Ottawa to the press gallery. And here is his story about Laurier.

On arriving in Ottawa young Dafoe was taken by an old timer in the press gallery for a tour around the buildings on Parliament Hill. In due course they came to the Library of Parliament. Sitting in one of the alcoves there, and reading intently, was a gentlemanly looking individual. The old timer drew Dafoe's attention to him. "Do you know who that man is?" he asked. No, Dafoe had never seen him before. "Well," said the old timer, "that's Wilfrid Laurier from Quebec. He came up here ten years ago with a great reputation. He was a great orator, he had charm, he had everything. He was the main promise among Quebec Liberals. But since then all that promise has been proved to be without any basis. He has been a complete disappointment. He has no future. Why, just look at him now. He does nothing nowadays, but sit here in the Library, day after day, reading books!"

And here is Dafoe's story about Blake. As the young Conservative Dafoe sat in the press gallery he was reluctantly impressed by Blake's long magisterial speeches. He listened to the Blake attacks on government policy, and no one on the government side seemed to get up with an adequate answer. "But," Dafoe consoled himself, "one of these days the old man will get up, and he'll answer Blake and put Blake in his place." The old man never did answer Blake, at least to Dafoe's satisfaction. Then one day, as he came down from the press gallery after one of these long two-or-three-hour Blake speeches, a flash of revelation burst on young Dafoe's mind. He had been converted to Liberalism by Blake! "And from that day," said Mr. Dafoe, "I was a fighting Liberal." Well, Edward Blake, as I have said, was a failure. But the man who converted J. W. Dafoe to the Liberal cause was not altogether a failure.

When Blake gave up the leadership of his party in 1887, he practically imposed Laurier upon it as his successor. By this time the two men had reached an intimacy of friendship which is almost unique in Canadian political history. There is nothing so nearly impossible in politics as for leaders within the same party to be genuine friends of each other. For they are all climbing the greasy pole together, and one gets up only by pulling another down. Blake was a reserved and ungregarious person, aloof from most of his followers; but beneath his cold exterior was a deeply passionate nature, and he was always longing for that personal affection to which he himself could so seldom give adequate expression. In his relationship with Laurier he found what he craved. From 1880 he and Laurier sat side by side in the House, they corresponded with each other freely, and they frequently visited each other in Arthabaskaville, Toronto or Murray Bay. Their correspondence makes a fascinating study.

I shall quote from only three letters of Blake written at widely spaced intervals. The first has the date 1891, a short time after Blake had dropped his bomb of the West Durham letter. This was published in the papers on March 6, the day after the election. Blake's insistence on coming out with a damning criticism of the party policy while election passions were still high so offended his Liberal friends that for several months thereafter not a single Liberal leader except David Mills wrote to him. He suffered agonies under this ostracism. Then suddenly, on July 19, Laurier wrote him a friendly note asking for some advice on a bill that was coming up in parliament, expressing the hope that differences of opinion on the trade question would not affect their personal friendship and adding some half-apologetic remarks about his own leadership of the party.

My DEAR LAURIER,

I wrote you last in the early days of March. Yesterday, long after all expectation of ever hearing from you again had died out of my mind, I received your letter of July 19. . . . I enclose you a memo as you request. . . . You say truly that you have often & sincerely offered me the resumption of the lead. You know that the position has always been distasteful to me . . . and that I was decided even before the recent difference never to resume the lead. . . . Neither of us has ever wanted the crown of thorns; & no question can ever arise on that head. . . .

I have little more to add. When I regarded first of all the course which the *Globe* & some other organs took, & when following thereon I considered the attitude assumed by my party generally, by my old friends, by those with whom I had been in close & intimate communion for so many years; none of whom have since the elections made any more attempt to communicate with me than if I were dead; who have treated me as one dead; I could not but conclude that I was in fact dead to them, & had lost their private friendship & personal sympathy as well as their political confidence. . . .

Not being the brute devoid of natural affections which some politicians have made me out; but a man perhaps more than ordinarily dependent for my happiness on my friendships, I am not ashamed to say that I have suffered heavily from this dispensation.

But time will make life tolerable, or end it; & meanwhile I am, with a heart which has never beat otherwise than warmly & kindly towards you, & which must love you still,

Yours Faithfully,
EDWARD BLAKE

By the time that Laurier came into office in 1896 Blake was an M.P. in the British parliament. But Laurier tried to get him back to Canada:

Sir Oliver Mowat (now Minister of Justice) to Blake 24 November, 1896
Laurier authorizes me to say that either of the Chief Justiceships will be open to you for acceptance when the time comes that appointment must be made. . . . In the case of your acceptance of either office, the other, if preferable, would be open to you when it became vacant. I do not want a present answer from you. I should rather not have a present answer lest it should be "no." Both Laurier and myself agree that such an appointment would be in the highest degree in the interests of the country. I need not say that you could have no rival for consideration as regards either. . . . I may add that I find our Premier has always had some hope that when you once more make Canada your home you would again enter political life here, and he is such a politician that I quite see he would personally rejoice more at your return to Canadian politics than even at your taking the Chief Justiceship of the Supreme Court.

"Laurier's wish," Blake wrote back to Mowat, "that I should return to Canadian political life is like what I have always found him." And while he felt it his duty to stay with his Irish colleagues in Westminster, he and Laurier continued their friendly relations. In 1903 Laurier appointed him chief Canadian counsel in the Alaska boundary case, a position which Blake had to throw up, after six months' hard work, through one of his frequent breakdowns in health. In 1905 Laurier again offered him the Supreme Court.

Finally in 1907 Blake was compelled to give up all thoughts of a further career, whether in the British or in the Canadian parliaments, at the bar or on the bench. A complete shattering of his health brought him back to Canada a broken man. For the last five years of his life, in his home on Jarvis St. in Toronto, he lived as a recluse, a more and more helpless invalid. The last bit of correspondence between him and Laurier that I have come across is dated at the end of December, 1909. Blake had had a stroke which left one side partially paralysed; and his last two letters to Laurier are written in pencil in an awkward, almost undecipherable scrawl.

Blake had had a young lady as secretary who had moved out to Regina and obtained a position in an office in the government of the new province of Saskachewan. She found her salary inadequate—it was fifty dollars a month—and she wrote to her old employer to ask him to write to Sir Wilfrid Laurier, to ask him to write to Walter Scott, the premier of Saskatchewan, to see if something couldn't be done on the salary question. Blake wrote to Laurier explaining the situation:

I write a reluctant letter because I know the pressure on you. . . . We have not communicated since more than three years ago. . . . I live a secluded life, but the limitations and qualifications of my disease which follows its slowly appointed course to the inevitable end yet allow me to think of the great business of our empire and specially as it concerns our own country Canada. . . . Thank God, though the body fails and I remain too long a wreck on the shore, my mind is as clear as I might well expect, and my wishes to my friends as ardent. So they are for you, Yours ever faithfully, Edward Blake, your old friend.

Laurier replied graciously but had to tell Blake that he had omitted to give the young lady's name. So Blake wrote a second letter (20 December, 1909).

MY DEAR LAURIER,

A thousand thanks for your very kind reply. The name of my correspondent is Miss A—— B——. . . . I am ashamed of my forgetfulness in not inserting it. But I write now only a letter or two a month, and what with disease and physical difficulties I make a sad business of these, as you may see. . . . I confess to you that for a little while I felt depressed at being out of the struggle in the old country, but my health fails. . . . [I have been] convinced that my career was closed & must remain a "carrière manquée." I try to console myself by the reflection that I did my best. . . . My wife joins me in new years greetings. I cannot hope ever to see you again. But I will not cease to think of you in your arduous struggles . . . so long as my (poor) existence endures.

Ever, my dear Laurier,
Your old friend,
EDWARD BLAKE

A little more than two years after this, his disease, following its slowly appointed course, reached its inevitable end. Edward Blake died on March 1, 1912.

The period of Blake's career in Canadian politics from the 1860's to the 1890's had not been one in which liberalism flourished in most parts of the Western world. The United States, after the strain of the Civil War, was plunging into an orgy of material expansion and political corruption. In Europe the hopeful liberal nationalism of the early nineteenth century was beginning to sour into the reactionary intolerant nationalism with which we have become familar in the twentieth century. Cobdenite dreams of a peaceful co-operating world were passing into the nightmare of Bismarckian power politics. In such a world environment there was little nourishment for the liberal spirit in Canada.

Blake spent most of his career in Canada fighting for a liberalism that was a minority cause. He left Canadian public life just when, in purely domestic politics, the liberal tide was beginning to flow. At the moment when he entered Irish politics, in 1892, it looked as if the Irish nationalist cause—a liberal cause, in Blake's view—as embodied in Gladstone's second Home Rule bill, was about to triumph. He expected to stay only for a year or two until the new system should be well established. But, alas, Home Rule was defeated in 1893; and Blake stayed on for fifteen heartbreaking years during which the Irish cause sank to its lowest depth in modern times. Then, in 1907, just when the cause began to revive, he was compelled to abandon it for good, because of his physical collapse.

What an ending to a career which had begun in such hope! What a contrast to those early years of the 1870's when Edward Blake had been, as Goldwin Smith put it, "the child of promise and the morning star" of advanced Canadian liberalism! By the time of his death in 1912 his name was largely forgotten in Canada. He had been a failure. But surely modern Canadian Liberals, in their present years of success, should acknowledge how much they owe to this noble failure.

MALCOLM ROSS CN

GOLDWIN SMITH

Why have our Canadian historians, preoccupied as they have been with the Confederation years and the early growth of our nationhood, dealt with Goldwin Smith mainly in asides, made of him a figure of the periphery, a footnote to our story? It is true he called himself, signed himself, thought of himself as "The Bystander." And he *was* a man apart. Reared in that proud home of lost causes overseas, he fought over here for causes which from the start had no chance of winning. None of his pet constitutional ideas—the abolition of the Senate, the Governor-Generalship, and the party system—has yet made its mark. And what has become of the grand continental design, the political union of Canada and the United States? (I suppose Goldwin Smith is remembered by most Canadians, if at all, as "the annexationist," the man who tried "to sell us out to the Yankees.")

But I am running ahead of the story. It is as well to begin any assessment of Goldwin Smith with the flat admission that he did not move with the main stream of our national political life. Our historians, with their constitutional and political bias (a bias which, I hasten to add, has been necessary and fruitful), can scarcely be censured for concerning themselves with the main stream. However, the Bystander has some advantage over the swimmer—in perspective. Certainly Goldwin Smith had far-sighted observations to make about the speed (and direction)

29

of the current. Thus he raised troublesome "horizontal" questions which no Canadian has really and finally answered.

Frank H. Underhill, in a crisp and just essay published in the *University of Toronto Quarterly* (April 1933) has this to say about his place in our history:

The problem of our Canadian nationality, of the conditions which have determined its development in the past, of the possibilities which lie before it in the future, is the fundamental question which confronts any student of Canadian affairs. It was because Goldwin Smith's mind was exercised about this problem for so long a time and because he brought to it such a store of experience and philosophy from an older civilization that he is so much worth studying. Why has the growth of nationality been so slow and uncertain?... The gristle of our frame has never matured and hardened into bone. As Sir John Willison remarked cynically at the close of his life, with every change of government in Canada we are made into a nation over again. And the student of Canadian history, as he puzzles over these conditions, gets an overpowering feeling that he is going round and round inside a squirrel cage. He begins to wonder if Goldwin Smith's interpretation of events was quite so wide of the mark after all. I expect that when the definitive history of the Dominion is at last written it will contain long and frequent quotations from the Bystander.

Surely it is high time to look again at Goldwin Smith, at the alien Bystander who pondered so painfully the meaning and motion of our nationality, and our North Americanism, and our traditional loyalty to the Crown (the Bystander would call this our "colonialism"). And have we forgotten that he was talking of Commonwealth as opposed to Empire well before the notion was heard of here? (How exhilarated he would have been at the birth of republics within the British Commonwealth—and how annoyed that these republics should be Asian rather than Anglo-Saxon!)

I cannot, of course, even attempt to discuss in any fullness Goldwin Smith's place in the political and intellectual life of three nations—Britain, the United States and Canada. An important, readable study of Goldwin Smith has been published by the University of Toronto Press. It is by Elisabeth Wallace, who very generously permitted me to read her manuscript in advance of publication. Miss Wallace's book has broadened my knowledge and deepened my appreciation of Goldwin Smith. And I have had to modify some of my judgments. Not that Miss Wallace should be held accountable for most of the things I am going to say. For I am, in any case, going to keep to the periphery of Goldwin Smith's peripheral career and speculate a bit about the significance of some of his ideas—and about the significance of this kind of man. But first I must also acknowledge the help I have received from Ronald McEachern's unpublished Ph.D. thesis (presented at the University of Toronto in 1934), a pioneer work, and until Miss Wallace's book, the only serious full-length study of our man. It is to Mr. McEachern and especially now to Miss Wallace that you must go for the full biography and for a careful assessment of Goldwin Smith's contributions to political thought, education, social welfare and, above all, to journalism. I think Miss Wallace proves beyond doubt that Goldwin Smith did influence us in an astonishing variety of ways. And one has only to glance at the pages of the *Canadian Monthly* or *The Week* to realize what it meant to have Goldwin Smith actively in our midst. At a time when Toronto was little more than a pretentious colonial outpost, the Bystander nourished us with the best that was being thought and said in the world. The debate on evolution, the latest literary quarrels in London and New York, advances in science, the great theological disputes of the time—all are in these pages, as are Goldwin Smith's informed and provocative comments on national and international affairs. A civilizing force if ever there was one! No other ten men together did half as much to challenge and displace the backwoods colonial mentality of those early years. And when the cultural history of Canada is written (in other words, when our true and proper history is written) Goldwin Smith will at last leap out of the footnotes and trade places with one or another overstuffed lawyer who got elected to Ottawa, made the Cabinet, signed several historic documents, became Prime Minister and lived happily ever after in Canadian high-school textbooks.

But it is not my task to justify Goldwin Smith to his Canadian posterity. My interest is in the Little Englander who wouldn't live in England; in the anti-imperialist who proclaimed that as a matter of honour and duty England must never give up her empire in India; in the classical nineteenth-century liberal who savagely opposed Irish Home Rule and (more politely but none the less firmly) the vote for women; in the Manchester free-trader who gave his open support to Macdonald's National Policy of high tariff; in the Canada Firster who sought continental union with the United States; in the idealist who vowed that "above all nations is humanity" but who believed fiercely in Anglo-Saxon superiority, distrusted all dark skins, looked a-squint at the Jews and blamed most of the evils of the Western world on the Irish; in the democratic educationist who condemned state support for schools and who even had his doubts about a public library system. (Did he not once say to Andrew Carnegie—"a novel library is to women mentally pretty much what the saloon is physically to men"?)

The contradictions in Goldwin Smith are baffling indeed. I cannot hope to analyse them one by one. But perhaps I can get at what might be called the "principle of contradiction" in his thought. Now I do not wish to appear in the role of detractor, or "debunker." Actually, I am concerned here with a phenomenon, or perhaps I should say, with a curious set of phenomena. The inherent illiberalism of the liberal mind? The blind, stubborn and inevitable dogmatism of the anti-dogmatic man? Or merely the natural human aptitude for self-deception? All of these, I suppose, and something more, too. Goldwin Smith was the child of his time. If he was not quite an eminent then he was certainly a representative Victorian. Not the stereotype Victorian, complacent in the faith that everything is getting better and better, evolving upward painlessly from precedent to precedent. Goldwin Smith was the uprooted Victorian—and all the great Victorians were uprooted men. Goldwin Smith was, intellectually, culturally, spiritually, the displaced person. Much more than any of our eminent nineteenth-century Canadians (Macdonald, Tupper, Blake, Laurier), Goldwin Smith is the figure, in the germ at least, of contemporary man. *The displaced person.* By "the displaced person" as symbol of contemporary man I don't just mean the refugee in space—the Hungarian come to Ontario. I mean the person displaced in time as well as space, somehow lost in the universe—the universe of things, the universe of values, the universe, even, of the self. "Liberated" man we once called him. But long ago Matthew Arnold, in a mirror, caught a glimpse of him wandering between two worlds, one dead, the other power-less to be born.

What manner of man is this? He is, as Goldwin Smith was, the lonely man. Lonely in an awful loneliness. We don't sense this at first in Goldwin Smith. Look at the people he knew: John Stuart Mill, Carlyle, Huxley, Spencer, Tennyson, Matthew Arnold, Frederic Harrison, Emerson, Thoreau, Longfellow, the warm-hearted people at Cornell—not to mention almost every promi-nent Canadian of the last half of the nineteenth century. There were always visitors at the Grange in Toronto. And Goldwin Smith was happy in his marriage. He gave and he received affection. He never really wanted for friendship, and there was that within him which could withstand the slanders of George Brown, the defection of Edward Blake, and even the cry of "traitor" raised against him on the streets. (I think only Disraeli ever really got under the man's skin!) Goldwin Smith's loneliness was not of the simple and pathetic human kind. It was a meta-physical kind of loneliness, and it had in it something of the dignity of the tragic.

The man was, of course, a wanderer and before we try to search out his restless spirit we must have in mind at least the broad outlines of his career. He was born in 1823, the son of a prosperous physician, and came up to Oxford by way of Eton—where he spent as little time as possible on the playing fields (good omen!). He was at Oxford when the great Newman con-troversy was still in the air, learned much about the ecclesiastical polity of the place and the time, leaned to the liberal side in his religious views and took an active, indeed a leading part in the reform and secularization of the university. Soon he was actively engaged as a journalist (and on the liberal side) in English poli-tics. His appointment as Regius Professor of Modern History at Oxford in 1858 was not really an interruption of his career in journalism for, as we shall note, history was for him a species of journalism. The outbreak of the Civil War in the United States presented him with the great liberal cause he had yearned for and, with John Stuart Mill and the Manchester liberals, he became one of the foremost champions in Britain of the northern side. He visited America at the height of the war and was completely converted to what he then conceived to be the American democratic idea. It is not surprising that in 1868 he accepted the invitation of Andrew White to join the staff of Cornell University. But despite his fervent Americanism and his distinct reservations about the dull, colonial backwater to the north in Canada, he moved permanently to Toronto in 1871. There were frequent visits to Ithaca for he never broke his ties with Cornell. And there were frequent and sometimes lengthy visits to England where he was again and again implored to remain and take his proper place on the larger stage. This he would never do, despite a steadily deepening disillusionment with the *facts* of the American democracy and an almost total disillusionment with his early dreams for Canada. In Canada he founded, or helped to found, or identified himself with, one journal of opinion after another— *The Canadian Monthly, The Bystander, The Week, The Weekly Sun*—not to forget those hardier plants the Toronto *Telegram* and the Winnipeg *Tribune*. Some of these journals he abandoned; others abandoned him. And the Bystander moved on to the next lookout.

One quickly suspects a restlessness, even a rootlessness in this career. Yet we must be cautious. For all this rapid motion, here was a man whose political *principles*, at least, remained constant. Goldwin Smith, as we have observed, could contradict himself, change his mind completely about this man or that policy. But, paradoxically enough, the more rapid his motion, the stiller he stood. Late in life, and after his tirade against the British attack on the Boers, he was accused of warming up "the same old ideas," the obsolete liberal ideas of his youth. This is his reply in a letter published in the *Manchester Guardian*, March 31, 1902:

My old ideas are that morality is the foundation of the State, that a free commonwealth is better than an empire, that unnecessary war is crime and folly, and that a great industrial nation, dependent for its supplies of food and raw materials on importation from abroad is specially interested in the maintenance of peace. A tidal wave of the opposite sentiment just now prevails. But I am old enough to have stood more than once on the dry shore where a tidal wave has been.

Goldwin Smith preached in 1902 what he had preached in the 1850's and what he would, one feels sure, have preached in 1957.

Tidal waves came and went—but here he stood, alone. At least this would seem to be his own estimate of the meaning of his life. There is truth in the estimate. But not the whole truth, not the most pertinent part of the truth. The image is over-simplified: the single just man, the lonely liberal justified at last as the curtain of history goes down. A nineteenth-century stereotype. Ibsen's *Enemy of the People.* . . .

There is more in the record, much more. I think we have to get behind the man's political thought. His political ideas do not change, but he changes. He never so much as questions the liberal principles of the 1850's. Yet he is sometimes a very illiberal old man. Now a principle is an abstraction. It is futile to study a man's principles, especially his political principles, in the abstract, out of the flesh. It is not enough, therefore, to identify and define Goldwin Smith as a Victorian liberal like all the others, sharing with all the others certain convictions about free trade, free institutions, free speech, free inquiry. In his basic political principles, of course, he *is* like all the others. Thus his anti-imperialism and his distrust not only of socialism but also of the more moderate features of what we call "the welfare state"—minimum hour and wage laws, for instance, and even the state support of schools. Goldwin Smith would have had no sympathy whatsoever for the liberal New Dealer of our day. Did he become in principle more conservative with age? It seems to me that he grew even more stubborn in his Manchester liberalism. Surely, it is the "new" liberal, with his reliance on the omni-competent state, who is the conservative. But perhaps in their political usage the words "liberal" and "conservative" have lost most of their original meaning.

My point, then, is that Goldwin Smith's political principles do not change. But Goldwin Smith does change. There is a fascinating process in motion here which calls for some study.

Now, if it is not true to say that as Goldwin Smith grew older he became more conservative, it is certainly the case that he became less hopeful about America, about Canada, about the realization of his dearest political ideals. And in these later years, as the Manchester dreams faded, he became obsessed with the religious question. One might perhaps have expected the old man, disillusioned by the practical impotence of his political ideas, to turn wistfully to the faith, to seek solace. Not Goldwin Smith. A study of his religious opinions from the Oxford lectures of the late fifties to letters written just before his death would reveal a slow but sure drift away from orthodoxy. Surprisingly, this movement away from Christian orthodoxy is accelerated in these very years of darkening political disillusionment—these last years of his life. Some might see in this nothing more than proof of the man's courage, and of his stern fidelity to the principles of free and fearless inquiry. One can never doubt Goldwin Smith's courage. But we are drawing closer here to a sense of the tragic cast of the man's life—and to what I have called a metaphysical kind of loneliness, the loneliness of the displaced person, *our* kind of loneliness. Now I am not going to be fashionable and attempt a portrait of Goldwin Smith through spectacles borrowed from Sigmund Freud and Jean-Paul Sartre. This lonely, alienated man, this "outsider" of ours was no monster of self-pity eating desperately of his own flesh. A decent Victorian reserve keeps us at our distance. We have to look for the shadow of the man's inner life in the outward mirror of his pronouncements on politics, on theology, on history. I shall insist, in a moment, that we have always paid insufficient attention to the strange and revealing *interplay* of his political, historical and religious attitudes. And I shall try, in a moment, to establish the significance of his religious thought in the pattern of his life. Meanwhile, please bear in mind my contention that in Goldwin Smith's last years the religious question is an obsession. And in these same years the liberal cause seems lost; not forever, because the truth will out, but for a lifetime.

So far I have said nothing about Goldwin Smith's view of history. And it would be impossible, I think, to appraise his religious ideas and, more important, the relevance and the inner *action* of his religious ideas, without some knowledge of his approach to history. Remember that he was, after his fashion, an historian. Here are Professor Underhill's comments on that fashion:

How Goldwin Smith conceived his function of professor of history is somewhat difficult to judge. His inaugural lecture in 1859 presents the honours History school as a discipline in preparing young men of the upper classes for public life. That it should be also a discipline for the training of scholars, of historians, does not seem to have been a part of his ambition. He himself never settled down to research, and he has left behind him no great work which recreates and reinterprets for us a past period of history. Sometimes one is bound to wonder whether he would not have been a happier man had he devoted his life to his favourite period of early seventeenth century Puritan England and anticipated the work of those later heroes of research, successors of his in the Oxford Chair, Professors Gardiner and Firth.

I cannot quite believe that Goldwin Smith could have become the academic historian, the researcher, the objective seeker after what actually was. Even Cromwell is not for Goldwin Smith the Cromwell who *was*. He is a symbol of the nineteenth-century liberal dream—a symbol of what is to *be*. In general, Goldwin Smith regards history as a repository of moral lessons. As an historian he stands betwixt and between two schools (and for our purposes two very significant schools) prominent in our midst today. Perhaps one should say that Goldwin Smith *vacillates* between these two opposing poles of modern historical thinking. Is it not the case that quite apart from the main line of academic history-writing, two dominant approaches to history have developed, approaches which represent powerfully clashing forces in our culture? The first approach is really un-historical. Indeed, it is downright anti-historical. It deals in "the uses of the past." It rifles history indiscriminately in search of moral reinforcements—good-housekeeping guarantees from the past to stamp on the latest product out of the Marxist or the fascist or the liberal factory. Oliver Cromwell made up as a liberal and a democrat is an early and rather inoffensive example of a process of history-writing which takes off with Victorian liberalism and reaches its awful zenith in the successive "official" histories of the Communist party of the U.S.S.R.

Far on the other side, of course, are the heirs of Vico, the myth-makers, notably Arnold Toynbee. Toynbee sees history as the textbook of a vast theology. History is revelation. The actual rhythm of event in time is of sacramental import and in submitting oneself to this rhythm one may receive the grace of vision. Toynbee puts questions to history almost as the Greek put questions to the oracle. But the liberal-partisan, the Marxist partisan puts no questions to history; he uses history to confirm *his* answers to other men's questions.

Already in his day, Goldwin Smith feels the tug and pull between these opposing forces in the culture. Consider his predicament: he has no real inclination towards the academic job of research and objective evaluation; he is, from the beginning, the liberal crusader; he will *use* history; and he will use it as a journalist, for the journalist. Note this revealing statement and emphasis in his lecture "The Study of History" delivered at Cornell University and published in the *Atlantic Monthly*, January 1870:

At present the journalist reigns. His pen has superseded not only the sceptre of kings and the tongue of the parliamentary or professional debater, whose speeches, predetermined and forestalled as they are by the press, are read with a languid interest; a result which the enemies of rhetorical government, considering that the pen is usually somewhat more under control and more accurate than the tongue, may regard with a pensive satisfaction. The right education of the journalist is a matter of as much importance to the public, in a country like this, as the right education of princes is in a monarchical country.

. . . A man who has been raised by the study of history and its cognate subjects to the point of view where the eye and the heart take in humanity, will not find it quite so congenial to him to wallow in the mire of party fanaticism. . . .

Sound enough. And I am far from suggesting that Goldwin Smith is mistaken in his high estimate of the journalist or wrong in his belief that the journalist should read history. My point is rather that by 1870 he has come to regard history as a liberal Bible which shows forth, in simple moral lessons, the progress of Adam from the edge of his lost Eden to the Paradise Regained of Manchester Economics and the American Bill of Rights. And, presumably, from the proper reading of history, the young liberal journalist will sally forth to talk down the imperialist, free the colonies, abolish the House of Lords and the party system.

Goldwin Smith, clearly, is a "user of history" rather than a disinterested historian, the partisan who abstracts from history such items as can be made to illustrate and corroborate his *a priori* doctrines, his own liberal creed. Indeed, in the last years

Goldwin Smith's thought became increasingly abstract and abstracting. And one detects in his later writing an uneasy undercurrent of awareness that fact is stubborn and unyielding, that time is as real as it is irrational, and that man is unpredictable, perhaps even unteachable. The Manchester mind if not confused is, at the last, confounded.

But the intellectual plight of Goldwin Smith cannot be pigeonholed as a simple case of the abstract kind of mind faltering and failing before the facts. For it must be remembered that at first, and for a while, his naïve partisan liberalism was complicated by a view of reality which was traditional, given, if you like, revealed—the Christian view. And, at first and for a while, even his liberal dogmas of progress and perfectibility were held in by the need to refer them at every turn to a Christian sense of the meaning of history. In his Oxford lectures on modern history (published in 1861) he not only insists that liberal notions of the day must be scrutinized in the light of Christian conceptions of value; he also nods approvingly at the myth-making of Vico (whose theory of history is readily agreeable with Christian thought), and very disapprovingly at the system-making of Comte (whose positivism is a repudiation of Christianity, indeed a substitute *for* Christianity). And if Goldwin Smith, partisan as he is to become in his use of history, can never take the path of Comte, or later of Marx (the path of a rigid doctrinaire materialism) neither can he follow the path of Vico, the path that leads to Toynbee and the comprehensive, quasi-religious myth, if not necessarily to the specifically Christian view of history. The Christian sense of history, so strong in the early writing, never grows into a Christian or religious *theory* of history. Instead, a vacuum opens and widens at the very centre of Goldwin Smith's mind.

This is now the story of a birth—the birth of our own dilemma. True, simpler (and less honest) men than Goldwin Smith have been spared the birth-pangs. They are all about us. Still-born but safe, untroubled by the cross-winds of doctrine, dependable, dull, unfruitful—we call them "sound." And I am not going to disparage Goldwin Smith in favour of such fellows as these! But neither do I see him as a culture-hero, a redemptive force in our tradition. Goldwin Smith is pre-eminently the man doomed to no destination and to no exit, the displaced person, uncommitted in the ultimate sense and therefore compromised in and by the immediate, the transient, even, sometimes, the trivial. My comments on his view of history are to the point, I think. For the man's view of history, his liberal political creed and his religious ideas have a curiously rhythmical relation to each other. I can only give here the broadest sketch of this relation (as it appears to me). And in so doing I am proposing a "working hypothesis" to explain some of the striking contradictions which appear in Goldwin Smith's later thought.

His religious ideas are usually put to one side and dealt with separately. And his work as an historian is usually treated "in passing." The political journalist has held the centre of our attention. My own view is (and here is the "working hypothesis") that the dilution of Goldwin Smith's Christian sense of the meaning and purpose of history results in an increasingly abstract habit of mind, and opens up a vacuum at the centre of his thought which is to be filled by prejudice *in the place* of belief.

True, his abstract liberal principles of justice and liberty, *in his statement of them*, never falter. But Goldwin Smith can be most unjust. He can vehemently oppose liberty. The fact is that the more "open" Goldwin Smith's mind becomes on the religious question the more closed it seems on practical political questions. Not always—the old liberal dies hard. But it is fair to say that Goldwin Smith's political attitudes become more unstable, more perverse as his religious thought becomes more heterodox. And perhaps I should at least hint just here that one master prejudice, a kind of idol, enters the open mind of Goldwin Smith and sits in the centre of the vacuum left by the departing gods. The idol is Anglo-Saxonry.

Let us look for a while at the "religious question." I am not going to claim that Goldwin Smith was ever the complete, dogmatic Christian man. As early as his Oxford lectures one can observe orthodoxy slowly dissolving under the acids of Victorian scepticism. This process of dissolution (intellectually it is a process of abstraction, as we shall see) is at work almost from the beginning. But only *just* at work in these early lectures. The man's main assumptions are rooted in a Christian orthodoxy. The tone and temper of the lectures are unmistakably Christian. Notably, the *Person* of Christ still stands at the crux of history and points the way. Goldwin Smith may already be half-dubious about the Divinity of that Person—as theologians explain Divinity. The acids *are* at work. Yet there is here still a lively sense of the living Presence of Christ in time, and an insistence that time somehow takes all its meaning from this Presence. In any event, Goldwin Smith is Christian enough to puzzle and annoy his free-thinking liberal kin—who thought of him as almost superstitious.

In the Oxford lectures he is, above all, anxious to reconcile his Christianity with the new liberal doctrine of progress. He is aware that Darwinian biology and the "higher criticism" of scripture together threaten the very foundations of religious belief. But the most he will concede to his sceptical colleagues is that a new but nonetheless essential and integral Christianity will again arise, purged, phoenix-like, of its intolerance and its worldly errors. It will be "as united, grand and powerful, as capable of pervading with its spirit the whole frame of society, as fruitful of religious art and all other manifestations of religious life as Christendom was before the great schism; but resting on the adamantine basis of free conviction, instead of the sandy foundation of human authority and tradition supported by political power."

Even the "dismal science" of economics must be understood in the light of the faith. "The laws of the production and distribution of wealth are not the laws of duty and affection. But they are the most beautiful and wonderful of the natural laws of God, and through their beauty and their wonderful wisdom they, like the other laws of nature which science explores, are not without a poetry of their own."

One must confess that he is rather glib in his accommodation of all the new sciences, including the economic, to Christianity. Witness his easy faith that "to buy in the cheapest and sell in the dearest market . . . is simply to fulfil the command of the Creator who provides for all the wants of His creatures through each other's help." Surely Bethlehem is further from Manchester than Goldwin Smith supposed. But I am not suggesting that he was a great theologian—only that, in the beginning, his liberalism is far from self-sufficient and doctrinaire. Progress, natural science, free trade, all must be referred to Christ. Goldwin Smith knows that such an attitude to these great new wonders of the age will

41

only provoke his free-thinking liberal friends and he admonishes them: "It has been said that Christianity must be retrograde, because instead of looking forward it looks back to Christ. It is not easy to see why it is more retrograde to look back to the source of all life in Mr. Darwin's monad." Surprisingly enough, Coleridge, the avowed foe of the sceptical and the liberal mind, is quoted in support of Goldwin Smith's own conviction that in any assessment of the intellectual progress of man it would be "irreligious not to acknowledge the hand of Divine Providence."

Then, too, in these early lectures one encounters a specifically Christian feeling for the brotherhood of man. Consider such a passage as this from the Preface to the Oxford lectures:

Christianity is not opposed to a philosophic view of history, unless it denies the unity of the human race, or teaches that any nation was disregarded by God and left out of the scheme of Providence. Christianity teaches the reverse of this. . . . 'God . . . hath made *of one blood* all nations of men for to dwell on the face of the earth, and hath determined the times before appointed and the bounds of their habitation; that they should seek the Lord, if haply they might feel after him and find Him, though He be not far from every one of us.' Could the unity of the human race, the providential character of all history, or the progress of man towards the knowledge of all that is divine, be enunciated in clearer language than this?

This belief that God has made us "all of one blood" is to become dimmer, as we shall note. Meanwhile, it must be recognized that the Christian assumptions of these early lectures, although they are central to the thought, are already insecure. In itself the need to reconcile Bethlehem with Manchester puts no inconsiderable strain upon an honest piety. And already an inclination towards abstraction is evident in Goldwin Smith's distrust of all religious authority, dogma and ritual. The Person of Christ remains, for a while, the centre of reference. But the Person is abstracted from church and cult—if you like, from concrete historical experience. The Flesh will soon be reduced again to the word—mere ethical idea, moral abstraction. Indeed this process of abstraction, of reducing the Flesh to the word, is to take possession of Goldwin Smith's mind. And by a painful paradox his need for religious belief seems to increase as his capacity for belief diminishes. One observes a restless, relentless search for an abstract religious formula which can give peace to the soul without insulting the intelligence. One by one the concrete, historical symbols of the faith are discarded. The miraculous element of Christianity goes and then, inevitably, all the dogmas that define and protect the *actuality* of belief. I should like to quote from a late work, *Guesses at the Riddle of Existence*, published in 1896. You will observe that Goldwin Smith has come some distance in his religious thinking since the Oxford lectures. Miraculous stories are quickly disposed of. Then this:

> The Incarnation . . . is the centre of this whole circle of miracles. Without it they can hardly be said to have a purpose or meaning. But since our rejection of the authenticity and authority of the book of Genesis, the purpose and meaning of the Incarnation itself have been withdrawn. If there was no Fall of Man, there could be no need of the Redemption. If there was no need of the Redemption, there can have been no motive for the Incarnation. The whole ecclesiastical scheme for salvation . . . apparently falls to the ground. . . . What remains to us of the Gospel? There remains to us the character, the sayings, and the parables which made and have sustained moral, though not ritualistic, dogmatic or persecuting Christendom. . . . The sayings of Christ would be no less true or applicable if they had been cast ashore by the tide of time without anything to designate their source. . . . A biography of Christ there cannot be.

In short, the Flesh is reduced to the word. The idea of Christ is abstracted from the Person of Christ.

You will say there is nothing unusual in such an intellectual progress—or regress. It may be typical of Victorian religious experience. But it is the very core of Goldwin Smith's personal experience. These religious speculations are the testament of a man who finds himself increasingly alone in a universe increasingly terrible to him. For he can take no comfort in the agnostic substitutes for religious faith proposed by the Utopian materialists of every dye. "How far devotion to the interests of the race and heroic or philanthropic action will be affected by the departure of theistic belief *will be seen* when the kingdom of atheism or agnosticism has fully come." He fears the worst. "We speak of the brotherhood of man as our great security," but can a real sense of this brotherhood survive a disbelief in the Fatherhood of God? He knows in his own bones, in the marrow of his own experience that it cannot. He has reason to know! "When the kingdom of atheism or agnosticism has fully come." It will come. He moves towards it as fast as his thought will carry him. And he moves in dread. He shrinks from a future which his kind of mind is creating, which it *must* create, and which it detests. This is his plight. It is the tragic plight of the displaced person.

The same devouring process of abstraction advances everywhere in his political thought. He remains the moralist until the very end but the man's morality is progressively more abstract and, if by the 1880's his political thought is warmed by any faith at all, it is faith in nothing further above ordinary nature than the good old Anglo-Saxon breed and blood!

It is, for instance, astonishing to what degree his admiration for America, even in the sixties, rested on a predilection for the abstract. The American constitution appealed to him, obviously, because it was *not* the foster child of silence and slow time but a conceptual fabrication made at the stroke of a pen. The dream of America which possessed him before he had ever encountered the fact of America, is the boundless Utopian dream of the doctrinaire liberal mind. In a letter to Charles Eliot Norton, dated May 24, 1864, he writes:

The appreciation of American institutions which you observe . . . arises perhaps from my being 'an American citizen' in sympathy more decidedly than you suppose. . . . For my own part, I have fairly thought my way out of social and political feudalism, and out of the State Church which is its religious complement; and my *intellect* and *heart* are entirely with those who are endeavouring to found a great community on the sounder as well as happier basis of social and free religious conviction. . . . Most likely I shall be more in my element, in some respects at Boston than I am at Oxford.

In this last he was very much mistaken. He was never really to be at home again, in his "element," anywhere. The less he could abide England and her traditions the more English he became. The more he exalted the American idea the more bitterly he had to deplore the American fact. And while he was the intellectual architect of "Canada First," he clearly had no sense whatever of the national feeling of born Canadians. He even seemed to think (and here, surely, is the abstract mind at work!) that Canada First, by breaking the bonds with Britain, would speed the inevitable political union of Canada and the United States.

For, he asserted, it was not "natural" to string a nation westward along an artificial, and ludicrously expensive, strip of rail. Nature pointed south. And by all the laws of abstract logic nature *did* point south. But the railway was built. And Goldwin Smith never quite understood why, anymore than he ever understood why French Canada insisted on remaining French.

As early as the 1860's Goldwin Smith had committed himself to what he believed was the American idea. The rest of his political life was spent in a desperate and doomed attempt to square the facts with the idea and, by a parallel process of the abstract mind, in an assertion of his Englishness in defiance of English tradition and English institutions. Englishness, Anglo-Saxonry, becomes, as I have already hinted, his ruling prejudice, an unconscious substitute for, a psychological equivalent of, religious faith. For quite certainly his ideal America is a large England, an England purged of its history, purged of its very self, the essence of Englishness abstracted from the fact of England. But the United States, like Canada, refused to be the essential England. Goldwin Smith blames the foreign-born, the non-Anglo-Saxon, for this refusal, this denial. Particularly the Irish. He was later only to exaggerate the view, first expressed in 1866, that "nearly all the evil in the United States has come from the South *and* the Democratic Party, as might be inferred from the allegiance of the Irish to them." And while, as I have said before, his liberal principles *in the abstract* never falter, Goldwin Smith, in the zeal of his religious Anglo-Saxonry, crusades furiously against the Irish Home Rule Bill (in this, alas, he was not the only illiberal liberal). Just as his liberalism had once submitted itself in humble judgment to Christian value (indeed, to the Person of Christ) so now it submits itself to the dictates of this narrower faith, Anglo-Saxonry. It is disturbing to find the Oxford apostle of the Christian brotherhood of man brought finally to such a view as this: "Two greater calamities have never befallen mankind than the transportation of the negro to this hemisphere and the dispersion of the Jews."

Even the grand design for continental union was a devout exercise in Anglo-Saxonry. For the entry of Canada into union with the United States would, he thought, help to maintain the Anglo-Saxon character of the continent by counter-balancing the

45

weight of foreign immigration south of the border. Conversely, such a union would overpower the French element in Canada and force its assimilation. "Either the conquest of Quebec was utterly fatuous, or it is to be desired that the American continent should belong to the English tongue and to the Anglo-Saxon civilization" (*Canada and the Canadian Question*).

Goldwin Smith was never really aware of how violently such a view went against the very grain of our nationhood. True, he was later to make decent gestures to the French Canadians when, by an odd paradox, they alone stood with him against Canadian participation in the Boer War. In his brave liberal protest against the South African adventure he was supported by those very *non*-Anglo-Saxons whom he had always regarded as the great stumbling-block to a proper Canadian liberalism. In his old age he even went so far as to say that "French Canada attracts by its simplicity, its courtesy, its domesticity, its freedom from American push." And one remembers his intellectual kinship with Bourassa.

Is it so difficult now to see why the man fell, at the last, into such radical contradictions, why he veered from an illiberal assault on Irish Home Rule to an equally vigorous (and liberal) assault on imperialist policy in South Africa, why he assailed the British connection for Canada and yet took comfort from the little English-looking garden at the Grange? ("Fortune," he said, "made me almost an England of my own in Canada.")

To point the moral I should like to put side by side part of a letter written to Lord Charles Beresford in 1909 and some excerpts from his late work on religion, *Guesses at the Riddle of Existence*. First, this from the letter:

For my part, you will believe me when I say that I left England too late in life and with too many cherished memories in my heart to admit any rival to her in my loyal affection. In everything that I have said and done I can most truly say that her interests and honour have ever been uppermost in my heart.

(How this would have astounded the tories of Toronto!)

And now this from *Guesses at the Riddle of Existence*:

The good which we do to others yields us a deeper and more lasting satisfaction than the good which we do to ourselves. This is pregnant in fact, and may seem to indicate the purpose of the author of our nature, *if our nature has an author.* . . . What is the life of man? Our little being is lost in immensity. This thought and that of the impenetrable mystery of existence are likely . . . to take possession of the human mind if the *belief in God* is withdrawn. [Italics mine.]

What have we come to? Religion without God. (Or should we say, the genuinely religious man who can no longer locate the object of worship? For Goldwin Smith *was* a religious man, the friend of religious men—as his lasting connection with the Baptists suggests. A religious man without religion drawn to the warmth of other men's religion.) And here is loneliness—of the metaphysical kind. A homesickness that is never finally assuaged by the little English garden at the Grange, by an Englishness without England. The displaced person—in space, in time and in the realm of value.

Goldwin Smith is a meaningful man—meaningful to us. He touched us only obliquely, perhaps. The eighteenth-century mentality of the frontier was scarcely ready to receive him. Perhaps we have just now come even with him, and with his plight—the last plight of the restless, quenchless, abstracting mind—the mind that empties itself to be open, and is wondrously and tragically deceived. We would do well to know Goldwin Smith. And as we grapple with the troubles of our proud and angry dust, let us concede that our history and our destiny—our living tradition— is revealed to us not only in Hansard and in Royal Commission briefs, but also in such wars of the spirit as this—wars which sometimes must be lost before they ever really can be won.

SIR JOHN A. MACDONALD

Everyone knows the traditional picture of Sir John Macdonald. It is perhaps the most remarkable achievement of that remarkable creation, the Liberal interpretation of Canadian history. Easy-going, convivial, bibulous, none too scrupulous, Macdonald is presented as the man who, above all others in Canadian politics, made himself master of the dubious arts of political expediency. In his own day, of course, this severe judgment took on a deeper note of moral reprobation. At evening prayers in Liberal households during the 1880's, his dread unuttered name was unquestionably linked with those of Satan's principal associate fallen angels. At tea-time, when Grit families gathered together for instructive conversation and the portrait of George Brown looked down approvingly from the wall, the master of the house could readily find some hideous episode in the career of the Conservative leader to illustrate the moral tale which he was imparting to the little horrified group of earnest Liberal youths and round-eyed Liberal toddlers. In those days and in those circles, Macdonald was quite simply the politician without principles, without scruples and without remorse. And although those days have long ago vanished, Liberal journalists and Liberal historians—the two groups are not very easily distinguishable—have combined to ensure that this lurid caricature should leave an enduring imprint on the collective memory of the Canadians. Macdonald, it came to be assumed, was a supremely adroit politician, with few real purposes and even fewer ideas. He excelled, if he excelled in anything, in postponements, adjustments, reconciliations. He was "Old Tomorrow," "Old Compromise," "Old Appeasement." He was, in short, the "fixer" in politics, elevated—if such a thing were morally conceivable—to a level nearly approaching that of genius. And, like all such time-servers who deal purely in temporary expedients, he could have nothing of any value whatever to say to posterity.

The portrait, of course, is not all wrong. Even a figment of the Grit interpretation of Canadian history can have a few grains of truth in it. There can be not the slightest doubt that Macdonald was a most accomplished master of the craft and mystery of politics. He brought to his chosen art great natural gifts of mind and heart, character and temperament; and he developed and refined them during nearly half a century of active political life. Every device, every ruse, every conceivable subtlety was instantly at his command. And yet he carried out his magical feats in such an easy, jocular fashion that he seemed more like a gifted amateur than a grim professional. There was always time in his crowded schedule for lounging and drinking, for good books, good talk and good stories, and for quantities of acquaintances and friends. He never seemed to be in any particular hurry about anything. He rarely got excited or angry. He never became morally unctuous or morally indignant. The incredible fact was that he actually appeared to be enjoying life! How could one take such a man seriously? And yet, for some strange unaccountable reason, he *had* to be taken seriously. The solidity of his achievements mocked the facile depreciation of his character. The bibulous party hack became the principal author of the constitution of a great state. The indolent procrastinator created a transcontinental nation in less than a quarter of a century.

The defects and limitations of the popular portrait are obvious. It is not so obvious how they got there; but many of them are ultimately traceable to what may be called the authorized version of our nation's story, the Liberal or Grit interpretation of Canadian history. This interpretation, like its more famous prototype, the Whig interpretation of British history, is a curious and complex subject which must be analysed in detail to be understood; and all that can be ventured here are a few very general remarks about its origins and nature. The bases of the theory, which are largely journalistic, were laid during the last third of the nineteenth century; and as a result it has about it to this day a grimly puritanical, unctuously pious air which recalls its mid-Victorian origin. Obviously the preferred politician of the authorized version is a sober, earnest, volubly virtuous man, whose generalized features unmistakably suggest the lineaments of William Ewart Gladstone rather than those of Benjamin Disraeli. Liberal politicians, from Baldwin to King—but with, of course, the single great exception of Laurier—have conformed fairly faithfully to this ideal. Laurier, like Macdonald, had style; graces of manner, a gift of eloquence, a flash of wit, were all his. But Baldwin's speaking manner, to judge from the slight extant evidence, was as earnest, as characterless, as humourless as even Mackenzie King's; and Blake, though he had great intellectual power and a real capacity for sardonic humour, could put his own followers to sleep with the tedious prolixity of his speeches. All of them were respectable, serious, weighty men—obviously acceptable provincial Mr. Gladstones. But Macdonald was not. Macdonald was a quite unusual Victorian statesman.

He thus affronted the morality of the authorized version of Canadian history. He also was never accepted as a sincere believer in its principal doctrine. That doctrine is concerned, of course, with the central mystery of the emergence of the Canadian nation. Canada, the creed of the authorized version declares very firmly, is the outcome of an encounter between the forces of nationality and British imperialism. Great Britain has always been the real opponent of Canadian nationalism. The only serious struggle which Canada has ever had to wage was the struggle to win autonomy inside the British Empire; and the progress of national development can thus be identified simply and exclusively with emancipation from British control. Canadian history therefore becomes the record of the stupendous crusade, mainly constitutional in character, by which Canada has ascended from the degraded status of dependent colonialism to the serene heights of autonomous nationhood. All the great Liberal leaders, from Baldwin to King, have been passionate crusaders in the good cause. Baldwin won responsible government; Blake reduced the powers of the Governor-General; Laurier foiled the plots of the

Colonial Office; and King effected his people's final deliverance through the Statute of Westminster.

But what of Macdonald? Eyebrows were lifted, lips were pursed. It was plain, according to the Liberal interpretation of Canadian history, that Macdonald was just as badly deficient in faith as he was in good works. He had been heard to say that the maintenance of a separate political existence in a continent dominated by the United States was the most difficult task confronting the Canadian nation. He had gone so far as to imply that it was American imperialism, not British, which constituted the real threat to Canadian autonomy. He had even had the temerity to suggest that the British connection, far from being a constitutional fetter, was a valuable alliance by which Canada could correct the imbalance of power on the North American continent and help to ensure her own survival as a distinct and separate nation. Obviously these were not honest doubts and legitimate questionings. They were appalling heresies; and on their basis he would have to be judged. He was certainly heretical, possibly idolatrous, for he had gone a-whoring after strange gods; and all that could be said for his political immortal soul was that he had shown a certain low cunning as a politician. In the authorized version, little space would be given him, little respect would be paid to him. A collection of amusing, slightly bawdy stories, a number of drunken sprees, a few unsavoury scandals, a gerrymander or two, a couple of railway jobs, and a shrewd ability to persuade Orangemen and Ultramontanists to enter the same Cabinet—this was Sir John Macdonald.

It takes a good deal of moral courage to question even the smallest part of this judgment. In other countries, the search for historical truth, the process of historical revision, is regarded as an important and laudable activity; but in Canada any irreverent inquiry into the official Liberal interpretation is frowned on very darkly indeed. In Canada, it is not necessarily assumed that historical truth is to be found in a comprehensive and careful investigation of the evidence of archives, libraries and men's memories. Historical truth is laid up, a priceless and absolutely untouchable deposit, in the private minds of Liberal politicians, Liberal civil servants, Liberal journalists and Liberal historians. And as the Liberal government of Canada has gone on from strength to strength and decade to decade, the majestic orthodoxy of the authorized version has grown. It may even be established, like the Church of England in Queen Elizabeth's day, by Act of Parliament. Already a national repository or shrine has been founded in Ottawa at Laurier House; and two eminent scholars appointed, whom we have the best of reasons for thinking of as the "historians laureate" of Canada. Should we not crown them, metaphorically at least, with laurel wreaths, as King George crowned Mr. Masefield, the poet laureate of England? They will recite the old, well-loved stories of the authorized version. They will tell our children and grandchildren how Edward Blake exposed the serpentine machinations of Sir John Macdonald and how Mackenzie King finally slew the hideous dragon of British imperialism with the glittering lance of national autonomy.

They will do it admirably, of course. Perhaps this is all we need. Perhaps this is all we ought to get. And yet I venture to ask Canadians to admit the possibility of another version, and to begin their own re-interpretation of the career of Sir John Macdonald. What they discover may not be simply a collection of old stories that amused their grandfathers and great-grandfathers. What they find may be a tract for the times, which will enable the youth of today and tomorrow to make a new Canada.

II

Any attempt at a reassessment of Macdonald's contribution to the national tradition must begin by a swift disposal of the bits of folk-lore and the worn-down theoretical stereotypes on which the traditional estimate is based. There is no point either in going back, as scribes of the Liberal interpretation usually do, to Great Britain for historic definitions of Conservatism; and then, after having proved that Macdonald's programme does not exactly meet the standard British requirements, ending up with the sage conclusion that therefore nineteenth-century Canadian Conservatism had no political principles. This kind of doctrinal pedigree-hunting, this form of ideological ancestor worship, is one of the silliest manifestations of the colonial mind. It is not necessary to trace an idea back through Edmund Burke to Charles I in order to prove that is a Conservative political principle. Nineteenth-century Conservatism in Canada is not what Burke and his successors and commentators thought it ought to be in theory, but what Macdonald and his principal associates made it in practice.

From the beginning Macdonald had never shown himself a very orthodox Tory in the historic British sense. At the start of his career, both his friends and opponents united in describing him as a moderate or liberal Conservative. He believed firmly in the monarchy, the British connection, the parliamentary system, responsible government, a moderate property franchise, and a life peerage, as he called it, for the upper house or Senate. He was, however, by no means singular in these beliefs, for all his principal Grit opponents cherished almost exactly the same convictions; and the amazing extent of their unanimity is recorded for all time in the Quebec Resolutions which formed the basis of the British North America Act. The old historic disputes between Whig and Tory, Roundhead and Cavalier, were never serious subjects of controversy in Canada; and the extent of Macdonald's detachment from them is indicated in his attitude to the very name Conservative itself. In 1872, when the first election after Confederation was approaching, he had got to the point of considering a new name for the party, though he realized that the title "Liberal-Conservative" could not be completely dropped. "I think, however," he wrote, "that it should be kept in the background as much as possible, and that our party should be called the 'Union Party'; going in for union with England against all annexationists and independents, and for the union of all the Provinces of British North America, including Prince Edward Island and Newfoundland, against all anti-Confederates. . . . What think you of such a name as 'the Constitutional Union Party'?"

It is this word "Union" which provides the key to the purpose and meaning of Macdonald's grand design for Canada. The basic Conservative belief that the nation transcends the group, class or section lies back of this idea of national union. It is here, rather than in any other part of his political thought, that Macdonald approaches British Conservatism most closely. It is here also, although he has been dead well over sixty years, that Macdonald becomes as vividly contemporary as any Canadian politician now living. The supreme purpose of his existence was the creation of a great transcontinental British North American nation—a nation separate, distinct and independent on the North American continent. He aspired to found it, expand it, develop it, preserve it and defend it for British North Americans and their descendants until the end of time. Others, of course, had had the same idea. Nova Scotians, Canadians, British statesmen, British North American governors, had suggested it or advocated it in the past or during Macdonald's own generation; and people like D'Arcy McGee or Alexander Morris were far more eloquent prophets of Confederation than he could ever hope to be. But that is not the point. The point is that Confederation was a political achievement, and that until a responsible ministry in Canada, which was the strongest of all the British North American provinces, adopted Confederation as a plank in its political platform, the idea of a general union was bound to remain academic and theoretical. When, therefore, in the summer of 1858, John A. Macdonald and George E. Cartier formally announced a federal scheme as a government measure, they made the plan of union a political reality for the first time.

At this stage, and until the achievement of Confederation in 1867, the scheme was primarily political in character. It was governed by two main principles, the idea of comprehension and the idea of strength. The plan of union which Macdonald proposed was intended, from the first, to embrace not merely all the existing politically organized colonies, Canada, Nova Scotia, New Brunswick, Prince Edward Island and Newfoundland, but also the immense politically unorganized territories of the Hudson's Bay Company. A nation which included the whole of the still enormous British inheritance in northern North America, would be impressively vast in extent. It was also intended—and this was the second principle of the plan—to be equally exceptional in strength. Three years before the opening of the American Civil War, Macdonald, Cartier and Galt, the principal authors of the proposals of 1858, had drawn what seemed to them to be the only possible constitutional moral from the deepening political schism in the United States. As they saw it, it was states' rights and regional divisions which were dragging the great republic through weakening quarrels towards probable ruin. And they determined to make their projected British North American

54

federation as strong as it was comprehensive. Other people in the colonies, at this time and a little later, were considering regional unions, or decentralized regional federations. Macdonald never showed any interest in either. And in the end he was able to win the support of most of the principal leaders of the period— Cartier, Brown, Tupper and Tilley—for his plan.

This first, mainly political phase of Macdonald's national plan may be said to have reached its logical conclusion in 1873, with the entrance of Prince Edward Island into Confederation and the realization that union with Newfoundland would probably be indefinitely postponed. The strong federal constitution had been embodied in the British North America Act. The transcontinental nation stretching from Atlantic to Pacific, and from the river unto the ends of the earth, had become a triumphant reality. It remained to discover and bring out as completely as possible the economic and social meaning of this enormous expanse of territory. And this, in several important ways, was an even more difficult task than the political business of constitution-making and territorial acquisition. A half continent, well over three-quarters empty, would have to be peopled. Its resources would have to be discovered and developed. Its potentialities, about which the bitterest disputes were still raging, would have to be tested and assessed. How was all this to be done? Was it to be left to chance? Or was it to be directed according to some plan? And if a plan, what plan was the new nation to follow?

It was at this point that Macdonald determined upon the general design of the second, or economic phase of his nation-building. The policies in which the plan was embodied were not all adopted at once, of course. But the development of the scheme as an integrated whole did not occupy a great many years; and by the time of the election of 1878—only a little more than a decade after Confederation—the design was complete. It rested on a single, gigantic assumption. Canada, Macdonald and his advisers assumed in effect, was economically viable in its own right. Canada's economy could be organized, on an east-west basis, as a separate and competitive economy in North America. This was, in several ways, a more imaginative and daring conception than the original idea of the political union of British North America itself. The little northern provinces had had no reason to anticipate such an ambitious, independent, continental future. For generations now, they had existed as simple, staple-producing parts of great commercial systems dominated by metropolitan powers. They had grown up inside the protection of the Old Colonial System of the British Empire, contentedly accepting the benefits of its tariff preferences and shipping monopolies. And when Great Britain declared for free trade, and the Old Colonial System abruptly vanished, British North America sought and found an alternative preferential relationship with the United States, through the Reciprocity Treaty of 1854. In other words, before Macdonald worked out the national economic policies in the 1870's, there had seemed to be only two possible courses for Canada. She had existed in the past as a subordinate, tributary part of the maritime empire of Great Britain. She could continue in the future as a subordinate, tributary part of the continental empire of the United States.

Macdonald rejected both these destinies. He believed in the possibility of a strong, diversified and integrated national economy in Canada. His hopes were based partly upon the known and varied resources of the original eastern and central provinces and also—and much more importantly—upon the enormous potential productive capacity of the Northwest. The territories which Canada acquired in 1870 from the Hudson's Bay Company included not only the present prairie provinces, and the existing Northwest Territories, but also vast stretches of what is now northern Ontario and Quebec. This was the empire upon which his hope for the future was based. The Northwest, he believed, would in the end make Canada a nation. He clung to this conviction, despite the frustrations of the Great Depression of the last quarter of the nineteenth century, to the end of his career. It was upon this issue that he fought the last election of his life, the election of 1891, which is probably the most important general election in the whole course of Canadian history. And although he did not live to see the fulfilment of his hopes, the Northwest did in the end perform exactly the miracle he had expected. Under Laurier, who in all essentials continued Macdonald's national economic policies, and with the coming of better times, the prairies were occupied at headlong speed and put rapidly into large-scale production. In the first decade of this century, the tide of grain pouring like a golden river out of the west brought prosperity to Canadians and success to the Canadian national economy.

It is this which explains in large measure the extraordinary contemporary revival of interest in Macdonald and in Macdonald's design for Canada. In one very important way, we stand exactly where we did in the early 1900's. "The twentieth century," Laurier declared proudly, "belongs to Canada." There are not many individuals or nations who are given a second great opportunity; but the Canadians, the luckiest people in the world, have been given a second chance to make Laurier's boast come true. The first half of the century opened with all the encouragement of boom times. The second half of the century has commenced in an even greater burst of prosperity. And in both cases Macdonald's Northwest, the region upon which he staked his whole tremendous gamble for the future of Canada, has provided the rich sources of national success. Fifty years ago, in the first decade of the century, it was wheat: now it is the new metals, the new fuels, the new sources of energy and power. How shall we use these new-found riches of half a continent? Upon what national plan should we try to develop this second huge bounty of good fortune? These are the questions which should be occupying us to the exclusion of almost everything else. For upon our answers will depend not merely the course of events for the next few years, or for even the quarter-century of Mr. Gordon's report, but, in all probability, the entire future history of Canada.

III

Our interest in Macdonald is an indication of the urgency of our position. And our sense of that urgency grows in part out of an obscure, uneasy realization that we have lost or thrown away for nothing some of the valuable assets which he possessed. We are at once weaker and stronger than he was: stronger largely because we are the heirs of the good fortune which resulted from his imagination and daring; weaker because we have lost either the will or the power to use certain policies which he considered essential for the safety of our inheritance. A dim unhappy awareness of our predicament has been slowly growing in us during

57

the last few years. What, we ask ourselves miserably, can have happened? We were all taught—it was the basic doctrine of the Liberal interpretation—that national progress was to be identified solely with emancipation from British control. We all believed that once the great crusade against British imperialism was won, we would ascend unimpeded to the serene and spacious uplands of nationhood. It has not worked out quite that way. The uplands of nationhood have turned out to be, not serene and spacious, but troubled and restricted. And a whole generation of Canadians has been reaching the angry conclusion that it has been deceived.

Macdonald was not deceived. He realized that the nation which he hoped to create, strong and united both economically and politically, had a double task to perform. There were two goals of nationhood, not one. Canada must, in the first place, maintain a separate political existence on the North American continent; and in the second, she must achieve autonomy inside the British Empire-Commonwealth. Obviously the first national objective was the more basic and therefore the more important. It was also the more difficult to achieve; for the North American continent was dominated by the United States and, of the two imperialisms, American and British, the former was by far the more dangerous. It was upon these broad considerations that Macdonald based his foreign policy. A rough balance of power within the English-speaking world seemed essential to him to ensure Canada's survival. The diplomatic and military support of Great Britain could alone offset the political preponderance of the United States; and Macdonald proposed therefore to bring in the old world to redress the balance of the new. The Anglo-Canadian entente became the foundation of his foreign policy.

It goes without saying that, in the authorized version of Canadian history, this policy has been consistently misinterpreted. Macdonald has usually been called "an imperialist"; his party has been described as "the party of fervent imperial loyalty." These words and phrases mean, of course, exactly nothing; they are simply the Canadian equivalent of modern Communist abuse. Macdonald's whole plan for Canada was essentially nationalist; every policy, political or economic, was conceived as a means to the same great nationalist goal. At Halifax, at a dinner held in

September 1864, just after the Charlottetown Conference, he spoke of "founding a great British Monarchy" in North America. He tried, in the first Canadian draft of the British North America Act, to name the country he was creating "the Kingdom of Canada." And in later years he repeatedly referred to the Dominion, in language which was unusual for the time, as a separate, "auxiliary" kingdom. His view of the Empire-Commonwealth was instinctively the pluralistic view to which we have become accustomed in modern times. He was convinced, long before Confederation was achieved, that the relationship of Great Britain and Canada was rapidly changing in character. In the past it had been a connection of subordination and dependence. It was becoming an association of equals or near equals. It would be, in his own words, "a healthy and cordial alliance."

It is this word "alliance" which is the key to Macdonald's conception of the Commonwealth relationship. He hoped and believed, with all his heart, that Canada would forever remain a kingdom under the British Crown; but for him the vital reality underlying the formal association of the Empire-Commonwealth was the Anglo-Canadian entente. The word "alliance" was frequently on his lips. He took its terms very seriously. He believed that it should be expressed in fairly definite agreements between the two governments. In 1865, just before Confederation, when the question of British North American defence was up for discussion in England, and again in 1871, when the imperial garrisons were recalled from central Canada, Macdonald obtained pledges from the British government promising military assistance to the limit in support of Canada in the event of a war with the United States. Afterwards he always referred proudly to these agreements as "treaties"; and there is no doubt he believed that similar arrangements or "treaties" must regulate any contribution that Canada might make in the future to the defence of British interests overseas. Such a contribution, of course, was never made during his lifetime. He was convinced that, while the Dominion was in the formative stages of development, the whole force of the Anglo-Canadian entente must be placed in support of Canada's weak position in North America.

It was not until the twentieth century, when his design for a transcontinental Dominion had become a reality, that his successor, Sir Robert Borden, felt strong enough to extend the operation of the alliance to Europe. Borden held fast to Macdonald's conception of the entente. He offered contributions to Great Britain's European defences in return for a voice in the determination of Commonwealth foreign policy. And the place which he secured in the Imperial War Cabinet and in the British Empire delegation to the Peace Conference gave Canada an authority and an influence in world affairs which was commensurate with the sacrifices she had made in the First World War. The ambit of the alliance had been enormously enlarged; but it had been kept true to the principles that Macdonald had laid down. It was an alliance of kingdoms, formally expressed in agreements and institutions, with benefits on each side, and shared responsibility and power. It had begun as an alliance for the defence of Canada in North America. It had become an alliance for the assertion and protection of Canadian interests in the world at large.

In the brief space of a quarter-century, this alliance, in both its European and its North American aspects, was abandoned by Mackenzie King. King could hardly have chosen a more inappropriate moment in which to let it go. The first half of the twentieth century witnessed a persistent decline in the power of Great Britain. It saw an even more impressive and steady rise in the preponderating authority of the United States. The imbalance of power in the English-speaking world, the overwhelming influence of the United States in the Americas, grew increasingly obvious; but King, with an old man's obsession with the now antiquated and meaningless cause of autonomy inside the British Empire, chose this particular time to cut us off from necessary associations with Great Britain and to plunge us deeper and deeper into continental commitments with the United States. If he had wished to do so, he might in 1939 have forced the creation of a Commonwealth Council which would have given Canada a voice in the conduct of the war in Europe and support in defence arrangements with the United States in North America. He repudiated the very idea of such a body. With his mind in the past, he regarded any formal association with Great Britain as "imperial centralization." He preferred to let the United States and Great Britain run the war in Europe. He preferred to do his own negotiating in North America. And whereas Macdonald negotiated from positions of relative strength, King negotiated from positions of serious weakness, and—we are told by those who ought to know best—in a spirit of ready compliance. The result has been the series of discreet, informal bargains with the United States which, since 1940, has been one of the most distinctive features of Canadian foreign policy.

It is this which has filled the Canadian people with misgiving and apprehension. It is this which has awakened a new interest in Macdonald and his national Canadian design. Macdonald's prime purpose was to found a transcontinental nation which would have a separate and autonomous existence in North America. His fundamental aim was to protect Canada from the dangers of continentalism; and it is the dangers of continentalism, economic, political, military, which now seem to be pressing in upon us steadily and from every side. We are worried today, as we never were before, about the ownership of our strategic raw materials, our metals, our new sources of fuel and power. We have a resentful feeling that we are overpersuaded into an unwelcome arrangement about the St. Lawrence Seaway, which we are now trying to rectify by additional expenditures of our own; and we have an uneasy suspicion that the unpublicized negotiations which are going forward about the Columbia River will end in some serious reduction or abandonment of our unquestionable rights. Under persuasion which may very well be heavy pressure, are we being fitted smoothly and permanently into a continental capitalist organization, a continental power grid, a continental defence system? In Europe, NATO is a collective defensive enterprise; but in North America it is a two-power organization in which Canada can accept only the assistance, and the direction, of the United States. In the north, Americans build and man our radar installations; and in the east, in Newfoundland and Labrador, they hold and occupy military bases. The foreigner sits firmly astride the eastern approaches to our country; and the base, a primitive form of military imperialism, grimly questions Canada's claim to control her own destiny.

It is this sense of the danger overshadowing the main purpose of our existence which has brought Canadians back with interest and with almost the excitement of rediscovery to Sir John Macdonald. Perhaps the concern of these anxious Canadians is justified; but they should realize that, in the eyes of the teachers of the authorized version, they have behaved deplorably in yielding to it. The *Winnipeg Free Press* is an august guardian of the Liberal interpretations of Canadian history; and one of its reviewers has recently and magisterially denounced what he calls "the vain and blundering attempts of some Canadians" to convert Macdonald's life into a tract for the times. It is all right, he implies, for us to remember "the meddlesome arrogance of the British government"; but it is very naughty indeed to dwell upon Sir John Macdonald's diplomatic battles with the United States. We should expunge from our books and our minds "these old unlovely quarrels which belong to a vanished past." And in the space left vacant by the simple process of historical rubbing-out, we should put—what? Why, of course, we should put "a few more picturesque anecdotes of Sir John and his wayward greatness."

And so we can end, as befits loyal Canadian citizens, with a lesson from the authorized version, appointed to be read in all histories, articles and speeches. We must never take Macdonald seriously. A few more whimsical stories about his weaknesses— that is what history should provide for Canadians as they enter the most exciting and dangerous period in their political existence.

ARCHIBALD LAMPMAN

"The night of February 9, 1899 was cold and still in Ottawa. Snow fell steadily and heavily. In a house at the corner of Bay and Slater Streets, within a few minutes' walk of Parliament Hill, a clerk in the Post Office Department was dying at the age of thirty-seven. His death at one o'clock in the morning of the 10th is, I believe, the most grievous loss our poetry has ever sustained."

So wrote E. K. Brown some years ago (*Saturday Night*, February 8, 1949). His high estimate of Archibald Lampman seems to me indisputable, but I should place more emphasis on the achievement and less on the promise. By the time of his death Lampman had done ample justice to his gifts; I wonder whether, indeed, he would have gone on to greater things; and what he *has* left us entitles him to be numbered among the four finest poets who have made this country their home and have found here themes for their poetry.

Archibald Lampman belonged, chronologically, to the generation of Canadian poets who first published in the eighteen-eighties and nineties. The appearance of Charles G. D. Roberts's book, *Orion and Other Poems*, inaugurated what has been called—perhaps somewhat extravagantly—the "Golden Age" of Canadian poetry. *Orion* was a seminal volume, and Roberts has some claim to the title the "Father of Canadian Poetry." *Orion* spoke at a crucial moment to the heart of young Archibald Lampman, a student at Trinity College in Toronto. In a moving account of the experience, Lampman later described the exhilaration which reading *Orion* in 1881 aroused in him:

It was almost ten years ago, and I was very young, an undergraduate at college. One May evening somebody lent me "Orion and Other Poems" then recently published. Like most of the young fellows about me, I had been under the depressing conviction that we were situated hopelessly on the outskirts of civilization, where no art and no literature could be, and that it was useless to expect that anything great could be done by any of our companions, still more useless to expect that we could do it ourselves. I sat up most of the night reading and re-reading "Orion" in a state of the wildest excitement and when I went to bed I could not sleep. It seemed to me a wonderful thing that such work could be done by a Canadian, by a young man, one of ourselves. It was like a voice from some new paradise of art, calling to us to be up and doing. A little after sunrise I got up and went out into the college grounds. The air, I remember, was full of the odour and cool sunshine of the spring morning. The dew was thick upon the grass, all the birds of our Maytime seemed to be singing in the oaks, and there were even a few adder tongues and trilliums still blooming on the slope of the little ravine. But everything was transfigured for me beyond description, bathed in an old world radiance of beauty. . . . I have never forgotten that morning, and its influence has always remained with me. [*Lyrics of Earth* (Toronto: Musson, 1925), pp. 8–9.]

Lampman was excited and incited by Roberts, and he in turn was to afford a literary stimulus to Duncan Campbell Scott. "It never occurred to me," Scott wrote late in his career, "to write a line of prose or verse until I was about twenty-five—and after I had met Archibald Lampman" (From *Selected Poems of Archibald Lampman*, edited by D. C. Scott [Toronto: Ryerson, 1951], p. xiv). In Ottawa during the 1880's Scott, Lampman and William Wilfred Campbell talked and wrote about the prospects for a Canadian literature. Bliss Carman's career as a poet, too, opened under the encouragement of Roberts, his cousin and fellow-Maritimer. Lampman's work first appeared in print—apart from the college magazine—when two of his poems were published by Roberts, who was briefly editor of *The Week*, until he could no longer contain his chagrin at serving as a "stalking-horse" for Goldwin Smith's annexationist ideas. (Letter to Carman, February 28, 1884, quoted in E. M.

Pomeroy, *Sir Charles G. D. Roberts: A Biography* [Toronto: Ryerson, 1943], p. 51.) It was, in truth, a fruitful era. All these poets—Roberts, Lampman, Scott, Campbell, Carman—and with them should be named Isabella Valancy Crawford, George Frederick Cameron, Frederick George Scott, Francis Sherman and W. H. Drummond—brought out books of verse which, by 1893, when the Dominion had just completed its first quarter-century as a confederated nation, might be regarded as constituting a small shelfful of authentic Canadian poetry. Among these writings none surpassed—and few equalled—those of Lampman.

II

Archibald Lampman lived his sixteen years of life as a poet in Ottawa. He was born, in 1861, in the rectory of Trinity Church in Morpeth, Ontario, was educated at Mr. Barron's school at Gore's Landing on Rice Lake, at the Cobourg Collegiate Institute, at Trinity College School in Port Hope, and at Trinity College in Toronto. Those college years were gay and companionable —with songs, beer, tobacco, lively talk, youthful *camaraderie*, the editing of the College magazine *Rouge et Noir*, and practical jokes on Trinity professors—who were made up of erudition, myopia and absent-mindedness in the proportions deemed suitable in that era. In 1882, he was graduated with second-class honours in Classics. In the autumn of 1882 he served as a teacher at Orangeville High School. His failure as a pedagogue was conclusive by Christmas time, and he joyfully said farewell to his unruly classes in Latin, Greek, English, History and German. Then he turned, at the age of twenty-one, to Ottawa and the haven of the Canadian civil service. He obtained a post in the good old way: through a college friend whose father was Postmaster-General. There is no denying that, in a professional sense, his work in the civil service had little significance for Lampman. To the end of his days in the Post Office Department it was merely a job which provided him with a miserable income and criss-crossed his life with the inflexible pattern of routine. He never tasted, and probably never yearned for, such satisfactions as his friend Duncan Campbell Scott in the Department of

Indian Affairs derived from the sense of bearing a part in the shaping of policy, of attaining promotions, prestige and power.

No shrines to Lampman's memory have yet been established in Ottawa. After his parents joined him in Ottawa, he lived with them and his sisters in a pretty semi-rural cottage at the corner of Nicholas and Theodore Streets—Theodore known to us now as Laurier Avenue—and, following his marriage in 1887, he and his bride made their home in a small house on Florence Street, later in one of a row of stone houses on Daly Avenue—number 369—and finally at Bay and Slater. Some summer months he spent at a farm "just beyond the Old Brick Yard near Hog's Back, on the other side of the Rideau Canal from the Experimental Farm." (*Archibald Lampman's Letters to Edward William Thomson (1890–1898)*, ed. Arthur S. Bourinot [Ottawa: 158 Carleton Road, Rockcliffe, 1956], p. 64; hereafter referred to as *Letters*.) Those "breezy hills and terraced meadows" of which Lampman wrote (*Letters*, p. 15) were probably, Dr. Bourinot suggests, near the site of Carleton University's projected Rideau River campus. Accordingly, it might perhaps be proper to invoke the auspices of the poet's spirit upon those studies in Canadian culture and history which it is hoped will be a distinctive feature of future academic endeavours at Carleton University.

One subject for speculation has above all others teased the mind of everyone who has written about Lampman. Was his fulfilment as a poet blessed or blighted by his life in Ottawa? Was he unendurably oppressed by the daily and perennial claims of his civil service work, a sensitive soul in the toils of deadening routine? Was his development constricted by the dearth in this backwoods capital of cultural and intellectual opportunities? Sometimes in after years, remembering his dead poet-friend and the adversities of his life, Duncan Campbell Scott would murmur in a melancholy whisper, "Poor Archie" (*Selected Poems*, p. xx). What had he in mind? The discontent and gloom, likely, which was one side of Lampman's complex personality, the frustrations and disappointments suggested by such remarks as these, in a letter of August 29, 1895:

I intend to stay here in the civil service about four years longer until I reach the head of my class. Then by hook or crook I propose to get myself superannuated. If they will do that (and I think they owe it to me) and give me all the advantage that the law allows, I can retire on a pension of $600 or $700. I shall get some small quiet country place and give myself up to poetry. I can make a few hundred a year by the pen and there is no reason why I should not be comfortable and above all free. It is freedom that I want. I am bound, I am suffocated. If I had the genius of Milton, I could do nothing. [*Letters*, p. 29.]

One wonders, however, whether Lampman's anguish was less occupational than temperamental. Such outbursts—and Scott must have had to listen to them from time to time—issued from the morose side of Lampman's nature, a habitual melancholy and nervous tenseness which might be construed as the heritage of the Celtic strain in his breeding. "Hypochondria" he called it:

You used to credit me with a peaceful serenity of thought and vision. . . . I am becoming morbid, subject to dreadful moods and hypochondria and even insomnia has bothered me a little of late. [*Letters*, p. 24.]

This is from a letter of February 28, 1894. Over a year later he was writing this:

I was so far gone in hypochondria on Saturday last that I had not the spirit to go to the office at all. I went straggling up the Gatineau Road and spent the whole day and most of the next under the blue sky and eager sun—and then I began to perceive that there were actually earth and grass and beautifully trailing clouds in the tender fields of heaven. I got to see at last that it was really fine and that perhaps I was alive after all. [*Letters*, p. 29.]

He was, it can hardly be denied, for hours, even days, at a spell, the prey of nervous despondency and a sense of futility. But these sessions of gloom were the price he paid for a particular kind of sensibility: the origin, indeed, of his poetry. The wonder is that scarcely a note of this morbidity can be heard in his poems. Grumbling about the civil service, moreover, is nothing new or remarkable in Ottawa, and one may suppose that it will always be brought to its utmost pitch of plangency by a master of language.

But this was, as I have said, only one facet of his emotional life. In other hours, as his letters record, he was sportive and energetic, even at times exuberant:

. . . We have had some very good skating here—a not very usual thing in this snowbound climate. I and my brother-in-law, Billy Ross, skated eight or nine miles on the Rideau on Sunday last and got therefrom much physical pleasure and profit. I cannot play any tricks on the ice, can't cut figures and that sort of thing, but I can skate straight ahead with Berserker violence. . . . I have taken four weeks vacation and have spent it in climbing hills, and paddling canoes. . . . I am somewhat sore bodily this morning. I rode a bicycle yesterday (that was Sunday) morning and going down a steep place at a good speed got pitched over an embankment head first, —bike and all,—into a mass of raspberry briars—after that I paddled ten miles and portaged the canoe on my sole shoulders a couple of times, beside doing various other scrambling and hauling. As I said I am sore but have a good conscience. . . . I have been riding other people's bicycles and find it an admirable exercise,—wish I could afford to buy one. I did buy one for my wife and that busted me financially. . . . I wish I were not a married man. In that case I should take to running dangerous rapids in a small birch bark. Have lots of fun with a fair chance of departing this life honourably. [*Letters*, pp. 28, 39, 40.]

One is permitted, too, a certain amount of scepticism about the rigours of his duties in the Post Office Department. There are indications that civil servants of that period did not work under unremitting pressure. The hours of labour were shorter. One is struck by this remark in a letter of October 1894: "I take a run across the fields every day after four and so work myself into perspiration. I come back and take a cold dip. It has benefited me." (*Letters*, p. 12.) Ironically, such exertions could not have benefited him. They must, on the contrary, have inflicted fearful damage on his heart which, seriously weakened by a childhood bout of rheumatic fever, was to make him an invalid at the age of thirty-six and bring him to an early grave. But observe that recreation commenced at four in the afternoon. The office hours were shorter, the periods of leave more generous and the burden of official work less onerous. Most of Lampman's letters to his friend E. W. Thomson appear to have been written in business hours and on Post Office stationery, and it is difficult not to draw inferences from a remark such as this: "After a bit I shall send you down my *ms.* book in order that you may read the things I have recently written. There are quite a lot of them. If this heavy increase of office work had not struck me, I think I should have written enough that month to make a book." (*Letters*, p. 38.)

The decisive fact is that those sixteen years of his life in Ottawa were richly productive. Now and again his letters cry out that his inspiration has grown sterile; but the greater problem was that, for a good many years, he could not find a publisher for the poems which were accumulating in manuscript, many of them appearing in the magazines. Carl Y. Connor's bibliography lists the titles of 120 poems which were printed in the *Atlantic Monthly*, the *Canadian Magazine*, the *Century*, *Cosmopolitan*, *Harper's*, *Scribner's*, *The Week*, *Youth's Companion* and other periodicals between 1883 and 1899 (*Archibald Lampman: Canadian Poet of Nature* [New York and Montreal: Carrier, 1929], pp. 203–5). During his lifetime Lampman published *Among the Millet* in 1888, and *Lyrics of Earth* in 1895, substantial volumes both. Upon his death his devoted literary executor, Duncan Campbell Scott, added to these the poems intended for a third collection, and thus produced the greatly admired and widely read Memorial Edition, *The Poems of Archibald Lampman* in 1900. Forty-three years later E. K. Brown put together a small collection of thitherto unpublished poems and issued it under the title of *At the Long Sault and Other New Poems by Archibald Lampman*. Those sixteen Ottawa years yielded surely no meagre harvest. One wonders what of value might have been made possible by greater leisure, by emancipation from desk and city, if Lampman, as he sometimes dreamed, could have retired to "some small quiet country place" and given himself up to poetry. It is to be feared that he would have put in his time upon more of those tedious long narrative poems—novelettes in verse as he called them—which today are virtually unreadable. Or would he have manufactured a succession of monstrous closet-dramas of the sort which William Wilfred Campbell turned out so relentlessly?

The theory that Ottawa drudgery suffocated Lampman and robbed us of masterpieces he was never permitted to create is best refuted by his decision to remain at his civil service job in Ottawa. On one occasion friends in Boston, E. W. Thomson the chief of them, went to some lengths to try to obtain for him a position on the faculty of Cornell University. Lampman's doubts and demurs seem highly significant. When, at last, no professorial post being available, he was offered a position in the Cornell Library, Lampman rejected it. "I am becoming so imbedded in my present surroundings—disquieting as they are in some respects, that it will be hard to get me out of them. It will have to be done with a petard." (*Letters*, p. 20.) Similarly, he might have had an editorial position on the *Youth's Companion* in Boston, but

I doubt [he wrote] whether it would be well for me to go to the *Youth's Companion*. I fear, my friend, that it would merely mean passing from one frying pan into another and perhaps hotter one. Here the drudgery I do—and it is I must confess not very heavy—is a thing apart from my literary faculty and does not directly injure it. While at my desk the literary side of me is simply in abeyance. In the *Youth's Companion* office my literary powers would be brought into actual employment upon a petty and colorless kind of work in which I could have no real interest and the performance of which would require of me a distinct abnegation of all that is original in my bent of mind. A sort of employment like that persisted in for any length of time would be ten times more deadly than anything I do now. [*Letters*, p. 17.]

In this decision he showed, I think, instinctive wisdom. After all, professional duties and poetry are not incompatible. Some of the best poems produced on this continent were written by a lawyer, an insurance executive, a librarian, a psychiatrist, a gynaecologist—and, of course, several college professors. Lampman's life, I suspect, needed a framework. The image of the poet composing lines and even stanzas and sonnets as he walked from his home to his desk in the Post Office Department should not trouble our minds. In a psychological sense, it is conceivable even that his talent was strengthened by the stress between his hatred of office routine and the exhilaration of his excursions into the rural uncultivated environs of the capital. The constant need for non-urban experience made Lampman something more intense and specific than a mere suburban Wordsworth.

III

Ottawa was the scene of his clerical labours. But Ottawa was also the source of his inspiration and of satisfactions of several kinds. Highest among these must be counted the companionship of Duncan Campbell Scott. It seems to me that a special grace lay upon the streets and outskirts of the city when these two poets walked and talked together in the closing decades of the nineteenth century—strolling through Rockcliffe, or by the Russell Road to Dow's Swamp, to the Experimental Farm, along the canal past Hartwell's Locks and to the Hog's Back, or canoeing on the river, or even making little journeys up the Gatineau valley. Lampman owed much to Scott's candid and knowledgeable criticism, and Scott owed to Lampman the debt of a disciple: for, although their respective talents lay ultimately far apart, several of Scott's early poems, especially his sonnets, might almost have been written by Lampman. "Lampman," Scott wrote twenty-five years after his friend's death, "never worked in loneliness or without appreciation" (*Lyrics of Earth*, p. 11).

In 1891, they were joined by a third poet, William Wilfred Campbell, who, having resigned from the Episcopalian ministry for the best of reasons—that he had lost his religious faith—had hastened to the sanctuary of the civil service. Lampman, Scott and Campbell, temperamentally diverse, were drawn together, for a while, by a common profound interest in the craft of letters. They passed many hours of ardent discussion, either in the study of Lampman's house on Florence Street, or in Scott's sturdy red brick residence on Lisgar, or in Campbell's little cottage, "which stood in a small garden under the brow of the high bank of the Rideau River." (Carl F. Klinck, *Wilfred Campbell: A Study in Late Victorian Provincialism* [Toronto: Ryerson, 1942], p. 80.) No other city in Canada was to be so splendidly the centre of poetic creation and interchange of ideas until, in Montreal in the 1920's, a group of rambunctious and greatly talented young poets founded, and wrote for, the *McGill Fortnightly Review* and the *Canadian Mercury*. And I allow no exception for Fredericton, which brashly calls itself "the poet's corner of Canada." How much of their lives did Fredericton's poets— Roberts, Carman and Sherman—devote to that city? Other intelligent Ottawa men participated—such men as Alexander McNeill, Arthur Rupert Dickey, Nicholas Flood Davin, William Dawson Leseur, John Henry Brown, James Macoun and A. C. Campbell. Ottawa in Lampman's time was not, as some writers appear to have decided, an intellectual desert. Not that much intellectual nourishment, if we are to accept Lampman's view, was brought to the capital by those sessional migrants, the representatives of Canadian constituencies, who took up residence at the Russell House or in rooms in private homes while the householders withdrew for the winter months to their garrets. Carl Y. Connor's biography of Lampman, published about thirty years ago, is in many ways inadequate, but it was based upon Connor's conversations and correspondence with Ottawans who had been acquaintances of Lampman; and their testimony makes unmistakably clear that Lampman and his friends in Ottawa in the eighties and nineties were concerned about the issues and topics which were the concern of the rest of the civilized world.

Lampman's, Scott's and Campbell's views on many of these topics and issues can be read by the student patient enough to ransack the sixty-five-year-old files of the Toronto *Globe*. Almost every Saturday from February 6, 1892, to July 1, 1893, they contributed a joint column *At the Mermaid Inn*. One motive for the enterprise was to eke out Campbell's wretched income; since his starting to work as a temporary clerk in the Department of Railways and Canals, $1.50 a day was the limit of the bounty lavished upon him by the Canadian government. The essays which appeared in the *Globe* make plain what Dr. Claude Bissell demonstrated in a thoroughly documented article some seven years ago, that "Lampman was no pale recluse, but an active participator and an acknowledged leader in the intellectual and cultural life of Central Canada" ("Literary Taste in Central Canada during the Late Nineteenth Century," *Canadian Historical Review*, XXXI (Sept., 1950), 237–51).

No doubt, too, there were other stimulating Ottawa acquaintances not named by Connor, and referred to by Lampman only obliquely. Who, for instance, was the Miss Waddell to whom he showed Thomson's story of old man Savarin? "I think Miss Waddell's approval is worth having. She has a very good head and a very sound heart." (*Letters*, p. 31.) And can we identify the woman who inspired the series, "A Portrait in Six Sonnets," which Duncan Campbell Scott described as "evidently the record of a friendship strong in affection, and, to judge by the last Sonnet, high in emotional value"? (*At the Long Sault and Other New Poems by Archibald Lampman*, p. ix.)

Besides his Ottawa friends, Lampman—who, in spite of the

large element of reserve in his nature, could be companionable and gay—spent congenial hours with kindred spirits—having a "crack," they called it then—in Montreal, in Boston and Nantucket, and in Halifax, during his too rare and too brief trips away from home. Dr. Tait Mackenzie of Montreal was a valuable friend. And what of the Montreal painter Edmond Dyonnet? During a carefree week as guest of a group of bachelors at 913 Dorchester Street in Montreal, so Connor relates (p. 193), Lampman "posed for Dyonnet's pictures." Where are those pictures? Is it possible that we have not yet laid eyes upon the best available likeness of Archibald Lampman?

One more friendship must be recorded: that of Edward William Thomson, editor, during the nineties, of the *Youth's Companion* in Boston; and, above all, the letters of Thomson, which —again and again Lampman assured him—brought a special radiance into his Ottawa existence. All students of Canadian literature, and most especially devotees of Lampman, are greatly in the debt of Dr. Arthur Bourinot, who has made accessible generous extracts from Lampman's letters to Thomson.

At the centre of the circle of affection which enclosed Lampman were his family: his wife, his daughter and his little son (their first son had died after only a few months of life).

IV

The city, then, meant routine and drudgery, but not to an extent that might cripple the poet's creativity. He spent all the years of his adult life in a provincial, sub-Arctic capital, but was not denied the stimulus of books, friends, letters, intelligent talk. And these are negative considerations, after all. Let us look at the great positive fact in Archibald Lampman's life as a poet: that, for the kind of poet he was, Ottawa was the ideal city— splendidly set in a countryside of surpassing loveliness and variety. I think that sometimes in our considerations of the claims of Ottawa to have been chosen the capital of Canada, we pay proper heed to the political, economic, military and diplomatic reasons for that choice. But we neglect the most important of all: the aesthetic, the perfect suitability of this city to be the capital of this particular kind of country. Certainly, the poet in Lampman responded with ardour to the beauty of the city and its setting:

Perched upon its crown of rock [in a Mermaid Inn column, *Globe*, Feb. 4, 1893] Ottawa enjoys uncommon and romantic beauty of situation. Viewed at a distance of two or three miles, from any point of the compass, bossed with its central mass of towers, its lower and less presentable quarters buried behind rock or wood, it can never be anything but beautiful, and as the years go on, bringing with them the spread of a finer architecture and a richer culture of the surrounding country, its beauty will be vastly greater than it is even now.

Even the air of the city exhilarated him:

A certain atmosphere flows about its walls, borne upon the breath of the prevailing north-west wind, an intellectual elixir, an oxygenic essence thrown off by immeasurable tracts of pine-clad mountain and crystal lake. In this air the mind becomes conscious of a vital energy and buoyant swiftness of movement rarely experienced in a like degree elsewhere.

It may be that to Ottawans, especially in midwinter, these paeans would sound a little exaggerated. But we must remember that Lampman was writing for the readers of the *Globe*, for Torontonians, who more than any other burghers need strong persuasion that any city but theirs may possess claims to recognition. And the allusion to the "intellectual elixir" daily breathed in by Ottawans was intended, no doubt, to offset the Toronto image of a capital city smothered under the ceaseless driftings of snow, legislative oratory and red tape.

Lampman was not daunted even by the sharpness of the Ottawa winter, as appears in a poem which I shall read later. But the more moderate months of the year were his favourites: the months for rambling along the rivers, taking note of the wild flowers, lying in the meadows, gazing at the city from some pastoral coign of vantage. Here were the inspiration and the materials of his poetry.

The city—but only in certain circumstances: veiled by distance, transfigured by sunset, or transformed by snow:

Yon city glimmering in its smoky shroud . . .
["The Meadow"]

Still from these haunts and this accustomed seat
I see the wood-wrapt city, swept with light . . .
["September"]

The far-off city towered and roofed in blue
A tender line upon the western red . . .
["Winter Uplands"]

Far out to westward on the edge of morn,
The slender misty city towers up-borne
Glimmer faint rose against the pallid blue. . . .
["A January Morning"]

Faint and far off out of the autumn mist . . .
With the soft sun-touch of the yellowing hours
Made lovelier, I see with dreaming eyes,
Even as a dream out of a dream, arise
The bell-tongued city with its glorious towers.
["The City"]

"Faint and far off"—the far-off city. Almost always in Lampman's vision of the city the poet looks across the landscape or the river, across the distance towards the city, and *at* a distance which composes the city into a cluster of roofs and romantic towers. This is significant. Significant not only because the poet finds beyond the city the things that most satisfy his spirit: fields, birdsong, flowers, woods, running water, sunshine and shade, silence, solitude, and reverie. More than that: he repudiates the city as a community, the place where the pressures and pleasures of man in society are experienced. The city in those senses stood in Lampman's mind only for the ugliest facts of life. It meant the daily round, noise, the stench and uproar of commerce, human pettiness, human greed and anxieties—and these were not themes for his pen:

I too came hither, borne on restless feet,
Seeking some comfort for an aching mood.
Ah! I was weary of the drifting hours
The echoing city towers,
The blind gray streets, the jingle of the throng.
["Among the Timothy"]

Such repudiation of the city was partly, of course, an expression of his personal need for recreation—and I shall come back to this. It was partly Lampman's version of a recurrent, almost obsessive, strain in nature poetry from the onset of the Industrial Revolution down almost to our own time. But most of all, it was a deliberate limitation of subject-matter—deliberate and wise. Lampman possessed neither the sensibility nor the talent needed to make poetry out of modern urban life; as Baudelaire did in the nineteenth century and as T. S. Eliot has done in the twentieth. Urban imagery, material drawn from contemporary life, had no appeal for Lampman. When, as an exercise in literary self-satire, he wrote a city sonnet in the realistic manner and gave it the title "Reality" (*Lyrics of Earth*, p. 30; see also Connor, p. 116), he was fully aware that this was not, for him, reality at all.

Nor was poetic reality to be located in the realm of the intellect. To say of Lampman what T. S. Eliot said of Henry James would be somewhat misleading: that he "had a mind so fine that no idea could violate it." Lampman had a whole set of ideas— that is, views, opinions, convictions. This is clear from his letters, from the Memoir composed by Duncan Campbell Scott and from Connor's biography. Some of these ideas grew out of his civil service antipathies, some from his reading, some from his discussions among the members of the Literary and Scientific Club or the Progressive Club. Through the long winter evenings in Ottawa they threshed out most of the topics of current concern: the alleged conflict between science and religion, the hypothetical blessings of the single tax proposed by Henry George, socialism versus capitalism, the woman question. Lampman was even, half seriously, described by his Ottawa acquaintances as a Fabian—surely an audacious thing to be in Ontario in the eighties! A socialist in theory Lampman certainly was. "He believed" according to Connor (p. 83) "that Canada had a wonderful opportunity to give the world an object lesson in enlightened social reform by adopting socialism as a form of government, but he was shrewd enough to realize that there was probably no country in the world in which it would be more difficult to convince the people of the desirability of such a step." John Ruskin and William Morris were the begetters of Lampman's socialist notions; they and his observations of life in Canada in that post-Confederation era of enterprise and exploitation, the "years of Mammon and Might," as he called them. John Stuart Mill inspired his feminist views. Lampman outlined once the position of women as it then was and as it might become, in a passage which runs startlingly parallel with Bernard Shaw's thesis in *Mrs. Warren's Profession*. In a more general way, he denounced the inequity which marked the distribution of wealth in Canada, and deplored the spiritual sterility of those men who were dedicating their lives to "getting and spending," money-making for its own sake or for the sake of the power which wealth bestowed. Of the parliamentary system as practised in a nearby legislature, he had the lowest possible opinion. He displayed on this subject a touch of *saeva indignatio*. "The influx of party politicians when Parliament assembled" reports Connor (p. 109) "filled him with derision. Certain of them made him regret 'the falsity of the old theological fable of hell fire.' He said that whenever he saw them prowling around like blood-suckers and bunco men his mind reverted with love and tenderness to one of the most illustrious of English heroes—Guy Fawkes." ". . . Poor imaginative, patriotic old Guy. I would canonize him—'Saint Fawkes'" (*Letters*, p. 27).

There is probably in such sentiments a certain strain of personal resentment emanating from an obscure and underpaid clerk in the Post Office Department infuriated by phony civil service reforms intended to dupe the electorate:

Our just and enlightened government are just now zealously engaged in extracting the mote out of the eye of the civil service, regardless of that which is in their own eye. They have prohibited the franking of letters from the 1st of January, they propose to lengthen the office hours, to forbid men going home to lunch at noon; they have instituted absurd and troublesome requisitions in regard to obtaining leave of absence. In fact they are removing from the Service the only features of it which were an attraction to a man like me. All this, of course, in order to quell the country with an idea that they are reforming abuses and putting a stop to corrupt practices. I would like to see them smashed! I wish I had some knowledge of political history and some practice in writing about politics. It would be a delightful thing to have a hand in smashing them. They are a miserable set of rascals. [*Letters*, p. 12.]

This outburst came from Lampman's pen in December 1891 when the Conservative government under Sir John Abbott was reeling under the fury of an even greater than usual number of charges of graft and corruption.

Lampman was equally scathing in his views on religion—or,

at all events, church-going. By the middle of the eighteen-nineties, the Anglicanism in which Lampman had been reared had lost most of its doctrinal and supernatural meaning for him and had become a generalized feeling for the ethical decencies and an *In-Memoriam* sort of faith in the inevitability of spiritual evolution.

The day before was Sunday [he writes in 1897] and I went to church, a thing I do about three times a year. It always depresses me to go to church. In those prayers and terrible hymns of our service we are in the presence of all the suffering in the world since the beginning of time. We have entered the temple of sorrow and are prostrate at the feet of the very God of Affliction. . . . Sunday is a day that drives me almost to madness. The prim black and collars, the artificial dress of the women, the slow trouping to church, the bells, the silence, the dreariness, the occasional knots of sallow and unhealthy zealots whom one may meet at street corners whining over some awful point in theology,—all that gradually presses me down till by Sunday night I am in despair and would fain issue forth with pot and brush and colour the town crimson. [*Letters*, p. 41.]

One of the young Montreal poets, who during the nineteen-twenties and thirties unflaggingly disparaged the elder poets of Canada, wrote of Lampman in this way: "The pot-bellied serene Protestantism of Victorian England which . . . underlay Lampman's spiritual make-up causes us to chafe. We are impatient of reading into the face of nature the conservative policies of an Anglican omnipotence." (Leo Kennedy, "Archibald Lampman," *Canadian Forum*, XIII (May 1933), 301–3.) This was, of course, fantastically inaccurate. Lampman was not flagrantly British; he was not conservative or a Conservative; he was not, one might add, an Anglican. (Nor, I should add, was he pot-bellied. In point of fact, keeping his body fit was with Lampman almost an obsession.) Lampman was a radical, and his ideas conform pretty closely to the standard pattern of radicalism among Canadian intellectuals—a serviceable pattern, and a durable one.

But this radicalism, this secular liberalism, so stimulating of an Ottawa evening over beer and briars: what bearing did it have on Lampman's best verse? Directly, no bearing whatever. It was not poetically usable, by a poet of Lampman's sort. Valéry Larbaud's penetrating comment on Whitman is equally applicable to Lampman: "He was not intelligent in the vulgar sense of the word." That is, at his best he wrote poems, and not metrical essays on such topics as life, love, beauty, freedom, faith, duty, progress, man, God and destiny.

Sometimes, like other creative artists, Lampman misunderstood and misused his gifts. A Victorian poet without a message felt rather out of things. Lampman had no "message." If his poetry was to be a "criticism of life," it must be so by indirect ways and not discursively. Certainly, Lampman was conscious of the pain and muddle of life: "the weariness, the fever, and the fret," as Keats described it: the modern malaise diagnosed by Arnold: "the sick fatigue, the languid doubt . . . this strange disease of modern life." In a line of the sonnet "Ambition" Lampman sees the world and its tendencies as "a tangle of Desire and Memory" —a curious prestatement of the emotional emphasis of *The Waste Land*. Occasionally, he communicates a sense of inexplicable dread and bewilderment; in, for example, "The Railway Station." He was oppressed by the busy industrial life of late nineteenth-century North America, the spreading smear of the urban and the industrial upon the features of the country, the momentum of forces which he, like many others, summed up in the term "materialism." Out of such awareness came the poem entitled "The City of the End of Things," a poem which has a rhythmic vigour and unity of tone unusual not only for Lampman but for any of his Canadian contemporaries and most of his Canadian successors. But it is a *poem*, working, as a poem ought to work, upon the imagination, and not versified commentary upon society and the soul. I have in mind such a piece of work as "The Land of Pallas," the fullest account in verse of his socialist vision of the future, which as literature, however, is little more than a mixture of Morris and water. And there are such poems as "To an Ultra Protestant," "The Modern Politician," "To a Millionaire," "The Answer," "Epitaph on a Rich Man," "Beauty," "The Cup of Life," "Virtue," "Aspiration," and "The Largest Life," which are not without interest to the student—at any rate, the student investigating the history of ideas in Canada: two or three of them suggest a flinty strain in Lampman's disposition which is hinted at also by the set of his chin in the photograph chosen by Duncan

Campbell Scott as a frontispiece for *Lyrics of Earth*. But none of these poems, I think, came from the centre of Lampman's poetic gift. They belong to that rather large group of his writings which may be thought of as constructed rather than conceived, literary exercises in the tone and tempo of his sober city life. Picture him of a balmy morning meditatively pacing down along the leafy streets of Sandy Hill and up dingy Rideau Street, then over the Sappers' Bridge to the Post Office building at Sparks and Elgin, fitting into the frame of a sonnet or a set of quatrains some thought that had been hotly debated the night before among his friends, or that had occurred to him during his reading in Greek drama, a daily hour before breakfast, and arriving at his office with a rough draft ready to be transferred from his mind to a sheet of paper headed "Post Office Department"—on the mornings, that is, when he was fortunate enough not to have been overtaken or hailed by a fellow civil servant burning to discuss the latest excitement of the day: Edward Blake's emergence as an Irish nationalist, Goldwin Smith's most recent pronouncement, or Laurier's triumph over Ontario Conservatives and Quebec bishops.

This was the life of the city, of ideas and opinions and philosophical positions, not the life of his essential poetry. I am not denying, of course, that poetry can deal with "ideas." But Lampman did not have the sensibility or the stamina for poetry of the discursive sort, which calls for the powers of a Lucretius, a Dryden, a Wordsworth. No Canadian poet can excel Lampman in rendering a state of mind induced by prolonged contemplation of nature. That admirable poem "Heat," for instance, seems to rise in its close to a moment of vision, of special insight:

> In the full furnace of this hour
> My thoughts grow keen and clear.

But there the poem ends. The thoughts are not put into words. "Heat," like all Lampman's best poems, is poetry of almost pure sensation, a sensuous or nervous response to mood and phenomena. This was the limit, and the strength, of Lampman as a poet.

Lampman's last poem, finished on January 29, 1899, only eleven days before his death, was "Winter Uplands." The poem

80

shows no diminution of his power to render the impact of the actual—it is "intensely realized," as Duncan Campbell Scott remarked, "by the man who was so very near the end of all sensation" (*Lyrics of Earth*, p. 39):

> The frost that stings like fire upon my cheek,
> The loneliness of this forsaken ground,
> The long white drift upon whose powdered peak
> I sit in the great silence as one bound;
> The rippled sheet of snow where the wind blew
> Across the open fields for miles ahead;
> The far-off city towered and roofed in blue
> A tender line upon the western red;
> The stars that singly, then in flocks appear,
> Like jets of silver from the violet dome,
> So wonderful, so many and so near,
> And then the golden moon to light me home;
> The crunching snowshoes and the stinging air,
> And silence, frost and beauty everywhere.

In this last poem Lampman had made a significant emendation. At first he had written the last two lines:

> Though the heart plays us false and life lies bare
> The truth of Beauty haunts us everywhere.

But he was able, at last, to recognize his own genius. He cut out the abstract, leaving only the heightened impressions which cluster in the reader's imagination into a satisfying wholeness of effect.

v

And now to define—to attempt to define—the essential qualities of Archibald Lampman's poetic gift. I do not intend to make extravagant claims for Lampman as a "great" poet. He himself rejected the epithet, and in one of his letters evaluated himself with astonishing accuracy and candour. Not a "great" poet, he protested—in the face of his friend Thomson's praises—but "simply a rather superior minor one who sometimes hits upon a thing which comes uncommonly near to being very excellent" (*Letters*, p. 38).

What must first impress the reader is Lampman's unremitting fastidiousness as a craftsman. He never published a cheap or

careless line of verse. In this respect he has an exemplary position
in our literature. The companion quality is the exactness with
which he uses his descriptive detail. By exactness I do not mean
merely dependability as an amateur field-naturalist, though he
possessed that quality, too. Shortly after the publication of his
first volume of poems, *Among the Millet*, Dr. John Macoun, the
assistant director and naturalist in the Geological Survey of
Canada, wrote a letter to the *Ottawa Journal*, commending
Lampman on his skill in combining literary beauty with botanical
accuracy, and enjoining all lovers of nature to read Lampman's
poems (*Letters*, p. 70). Botanical accuracy in poetry called forth
the admiration of Victorian readers; you will recall the rapture
of the old gentleman in *Cranford* over Tennyson's "black as ash-
buds in March."

But Lampman was no mere transcriber of note-book sketches.
He selected and articulated his descriptive elements, composing
an emotional and musical structure of great craft and charm.
That is, he did so in his successful poems, which number some
fifteen or sixteen—and we should not feel that the number is
small: poets much greater than Lampman have garnered no
more from careers much longer and more illustrious; for by a
successful poem I mean a complete and unflawed expression of
the poet's distinctive talent.

These successful poems of Lampman's are, nearly without exception, the products and records of episodes of contemplation.
His images are predominantly visual: indeed in one of his earlier
poems he names as the very climax of pleasure the opportunity
to "drain the comfort of wide fields into tired eyes." His poems
are precise and variegated in their recording of things looked at
with care and affection. Occasionally, however, Lampman makes
effective use of images of sound. Surely, for example, the mount-
ing excitement communicated by "A January Morning" is
brought about by the contrast between the silence of the first
eight lines and noises of the last six:

> The glittering roofs are still with frost; each worn
> Black chimney builds into the quiet sky
> Its curling pile to crumble silently.
> Far out to westward on the edge of morn,
> The slender misty city towers upborne

Glimmer faint rose against the pallid blue;
And yonder on those northern hills, the hue
Of amethyst, hang fleeces dull as horn.
And here behind me come the woodmen's sleighs
With shouts and clamorous squeakings; might and main
Up the steep slope the horses stamp and strain,
Urged on by hoarse-tongued drivers—cheeks ablaze,
Iced beards and frozen eyelids—team by team,
With frost-fringed flanks, and nostrils jetting steam.

Another successful use of sound effects is in creating and defining
the sense of solitude. One of his finest sonnets is a splendid illus-
tration. Successive sounds seem to mark off areas of silence in a
scale of increasing intensity.

How still it is here in the woods. The trees
Stand motionless, as if they did not dare
To stir, lest it should break the spell. The air
Hangs quiet as spaces in a marble frieze.
Even this little brook, that runs at ease,
Whispering and gurgling in its knotted bed,
Seems but to deepen, with its curling thread
Of sound, the shadowy sun-pierced silences.
Sometimes a hawk screams or a woodpecker
Startles the stillness from its fixed mood
With his loud careless tap. Sometimes I hear
The dreamy white-throat from some far off tree
Pipe slowly on the listening solitude,
His five pure notes succeeding pensively.

Such lucid and precise evocation of nature is not common in
Canadian poetry—or in any poetry. The nature poet too often
blurs his effects by cluttering natural objects with metaphysical
and transcendental significances. Nature is made pretext for
essays on the Soul, the One, the All. Through nature, the poet
tries to get in tune with the Infinite. "Today when the birches
are yellow," writes Bliss Carman in "The Silent Wayfarer,"

To-day when the birches are yellow
And red is the wayfaring tree,
Sit down in the sun, my soul,
And talk of yourself to me.

The poet's soul, of course, accepted the invitation, sat down, and
talked; and that talk went on through many a stanza and many
a volume before Carman had done transcribing all that his most

83

garrulous soul had to tell him. Even a poet much superior to
Carman, Duncan Campbell Scott, could not always resist the
temptation to Emersonize in verse—and sometimes does so suc-
cessfully. Later Canadian poets put nature to work in other ways:
A. J. M. Smith, for instance, as a source of symbolist effects,
Robert Finch as a storehouse of aesthetic patterns.

But we must not mistake purity of execution for superficiality.
A closer look at one of Lampman's successful poems shows that
the effect of serenity derives from, and reposes on, a resolution of
counter-impulses. Consider a familiar poem, "Morning on the
Lievre."

> Far above us where a jay
> Screams his matins to the day,
> Capped with gold and amethyst,
> Like a vapour from a forge
> Of a giant somewhere hid,
> Out of hearing of the clang
> Of his hammer, skirts of mist
> Slowly up the woody gorge
> Lift and hang.
>
> Softly as a cloud we go,
> Sky above and sky below,
> Down the river; and the dip
> Of the paddles scarcely breaks
> With the little silvery drip
> Of the water as it shakes
> From the blades, the crystal deep
> Of the silence of the morn,
> Of the forest yet asleep;
> And the river reaches borne
> In a mirror, purple gray,
> Sheer away
> To the misty line of light
> Where the forest and the stream,
> In the shadow meet and plight,
> Like a dream.
>
> From amid a stretch of reeds
> Where the lazy river sucks
> All the water as it bleeds
> From a little curling creek,
> And the muskrats peer and sneak
> In around the sunken wrecks

Of a tree that swept the skies
Long ago,
On a sudden seven ducks
With a splashy rustle rise,
Stretching out their seven necks,
One before, and two behind,
And the others all arow,
And as steady as the wind
With a swivelling whistle go,
Through the purple shadow led,
Till we only hear their whir
In behind a rocky spur,
Just ahead.

This poem is, in its small way, a triumph of statement and suggestion combined. One may regret a few lapses in diction—Lampman was almost but not entirely free of the addiction to poetic language in vogue in the late nineteenth century: "matins" and "plight," for example; and there are two or three over-facile rhymes. Yet consider with what skill the reader is placed, imaginatively, at the centre of the scene and the mood. Even the word-order, which is slightly affected and anti-prose, helps to conduct him there. The poem—and this is the point I wish to illustrate—sets up a strange nervous vibration. Although the details seem to move, emotionally, in the direction of serenity and contentment, there is an ominous cross-current of suggestion. Something sinister in nature, some quality of ruthlessness, is evoked by the imagery of the mist in stanza one, and the "sunken wrecks of a tree" in the third stanza, and the associations of "sucks" and "bleeds." A similar hint or whisper of the ominous sounds in other nature poems. That excellent poem "Heat," for example, has an undertone of tenseness, almost the effect of hallucination. And that fine, sober-coloured poem entitled "In November" concludes in this way:

And I, too, standing idly there,
With muffled hands in the chill air,
Felt the warm glow about my feet,
And shuddering betwixt cold and heat
Drew my thoughts closer, like a cloak,
While something in my blood awoke,
A nameless and unnatural cheer,
A pleasure secret and austere.

"A nameless and unnatural cheer, A pleasure secret and austere"—the poet capable of ending in this manner an account of a November walk in the woods near Ottawa was a reverberator of uncommon sensibility. The flow of imagery and verbal music in Lampman's finest poems, then, produces an untroubled surface; but below that surface are interesting nervous vibrations. The result is a tougher poetry than its delicacy of texture might suggest. The undercurrents of apprehension preserve Lampman's poems from the too-frequent curse of nature poetry: insipidity and sentimentality. I would go further, and suggest that here is the key to the poet's relation to his poetry.

This is not the occasion for a thoroughgoing analysis of the personality of Lampman; although it would be a fascinating enterprise, and I hope to attempt it one day. I would lay stress, however, upon that duality of temperament which appears everywhere: in his letters, in the comments of acquaintances, in the reminiscences of Duncan Campbell Scott. Lampman would at times be gregarious and gay; at other times depressed and discontented. His letters record the alternation of moods. I do not equate this variation of mood with his twofold existence: as a prisoner of routine in the city, and as a poet responding to the charms of the Ottawa countryside. But I do believe that his poetry derives from the combination of the two rather than from the complete exclusion of either.

> I rejoice having to construct something
> On which to rejoice.

This is T. S. Eliot in *Ash Wednesday*. And Lampman rejoiced, soberly and in solitude, in the face of pastoral nature, not, however, as one for whom nature is the usual setting but as one who comes at intervals to nature to be re-created.

I was so far gone in hypochondria on Saturday last that I had not the spirit to go to the office at all. I went straggling up the Gatineau Road and spent the whole day and most of the next under the blue sky and the eager sun—and then I began to perceive that there were actually earth and grass and beautifully trailing clouds in the tender fields of heaven. I got to see at last that it was really fine and that perhaps I was alive after all. [*Letters*, p. 29.]

The poems are the verbal equivalents for that process of re-creation. Like a great deal of good poetry, the best poems of

Lampman represent an aesthetic equipoise that derives from a temperamental equipoise. Not escape from something called real life—"escape" is entirely the wrong word for Lampman's relation to his poetry—but the achievement of a vital interplay of impulses.

Without the lovely Ottawa countryside, interlaced by four splendid rivers, the poetry of Lampman could not have been written; for the poetry is the fruit of observation, contemplation—even, at times, what almost becomes assimilation of poet and nature. At the same time, paradoxically, the poetry as it is could not have been created without the city. If it had ever been possible for him to become a constant dweller in the country, in "some small quiet country place," Lampman, I am convinced, would not have written his best poems. He had to bring into nature a sense of a need for nature. He had to come as a townsman, a harried civil servant, a friend, a father, a husband, an "active participator," as Dr. Bissell calls him, "in the intellectual and cultural life of Central Canada"—in short, as a modern, city-dwelling man in the stream of contemporary life.

In the beginning, I rated Lampman as one of the four finest Canadian poets, the other three being, of course, Duncan Campbell Scott, E. J. Pratt and A. M. Klein. A Canadian poet. A Canadian poet who never composed a patriotic ode or a national hymn, who never once in all his poems used the word Canada or Canadian. But distinctively Canadian, just the same, and a part of our living tradition. Not only because of the fidelity with which he recorded his vision of one important part of the Canadian scene, but because his best poems came out of an experience which is characteristic of Canadian life, and commoner than we admit. Lampman's relationship to nature is our relationship. It is a relationship which, ordinarily, being Canadians, we are no more willing to discuss openly than we are to discuss sex or religion; and we conceal it behind a variety of respectable activities: fishing, hunting, skiing, boating, Sunday painting, getting away from it all for a few weeks, keeping the kids off the city streets in the summer, building beyond the metropolitan tax zone. In this country, we even conduct conferences in the woods and beside the lakes. But we have no wish to assume this silvan or lacustrine life as a permanent state. We value nature because we come to nature in an interval of our professional and domestic routine; fully expecting and intending to resume those duties and responsibilities, but with new spirit and new perspectives—"with new acquist of pastoral experience." In short (not to warp Milton further to force an analogy), nature provides the true Canadian catharsis.

This relationship with nature does not, unfortunately—or, perhaps, it is not a misfortune—qualify us all to write poems. But it does enable Canadian readers—and perhaps no other readers to the same degree—to recognize the authenticity and charm of Archibald Lampman's poems.

NOTE: Quotations from the poems of Archibald Lampman are taken from *Selected Poems of Archibald Lampman,* edited by D. C. Scott, published by The Ryerson Press who have graciously given permission for their use.

MASON WADE ON

SIR WILFRID LAURIER

The purpose of this essay is to assess, within a limited scope, Laurier's role in the integration of Canada's French and British traditions, leaving to some future biographer the weighing of what John W. Dafoe called Laurier's "affinities with Machiavelli as well as with Sir Galahad" (*Laurier* [Toronto, 1922], p. 15). My thesis is that Laurier kept all his life the pledge which he made at the age of 23, speaking in 1864 to the Undergraduates' Society of the McGill Faculty of Law: "I pledge my honour that I will give the whole of my life to the cause of conciliation, harmony, and concord among the different elements of this country of ours" (Peter McArthur, *Sir Wilfrid Laurier* [Toronto, 1919], p. 19).

What was the background of the young lawyer who gave this pledge as he stood on the brink of his professional career, and what led him to make it? Wilfrid Laurier was born in 1841 in the little village of St. Lin near Montreal. He traced his ancestry back through generations of French Canadians and Acadians to one of Maisonneuve's soldier colonists of Montreal, and to a member of the Carignan-Salières Regiment. Laurier's father was a land surveyor, as his father in turn had been before him. Carolus Laurier's recognition of the advantages of knowing English and English ways led him to send the boy to school for two years in the neighbouring Scottish settlement of New Glasgow, before sending him to L'Assomption for the classical college training which was, and is, an indispensable prerequisite for professional life in Quebec. Then young Laurier went to Montreal to study law at McGill, and to clerk in the office of Rodolphe Laflamme, one of the leading Rouge lawyers. Soon after being admitted to the Quebec bar in 1864, Laurier formed a law partnership with Médéric Lanctot, a leader in the anti-Confederation movement in 1865. Both as a student and as a young lawyer Laurier was interested in politics and in the new ideas which were coming into conflict with the established order in Quebec.

When Laurier began his professional career, Quebec was increasingly troubled by political and religious conflicts which did not tend to produce "harmony and concord among the different elements," and the prospects of conciliating these conflicts were not bright. The dominance of the Liberal-Conservative party, led by Georges-Etienne Cartier and supported by the English Montreal business leaders and the Quebec bishops, was threatened by the project of Confederation, which was not popular with the people. Many of Cartier's French followers feared the prospect of being left at the mercy of an English-speaking majority in the new federal legislature, while the English minority in Lower Canada was equally concerned at the prospect of being left at the mercy of a French-speaking majority in the new provincial legislature. Cartier had to use all the eloquence of a skilled advocate to carry the measure in Lower Canada by a narrow measure, and the struggle over Confederation eventually led to a realignment of political parties. Cartier finally won the reluctant support of the hierarchy for Confederation because they feared the anti-clericalism and republicanism of the radical Liberals (Rouges) who opposed the measure. But Cartier's alliance with Bishop Bourget of Montreal, the dominant figure in the hierarchy, was strained by the episode, and the way was paved for its breakdown as questions of Church and State set the political and religious leaders of French Canada at odds.

At this period Quebec was caught up in the European conflict between ultramontanism and liberalism arising out of the French and Italian revolutions of 1848. Like Pope Pius IX, Bishop Bourget had swung from an early sympathy with liberal ideas to a highly conservative and authoritarian position as attacks upon the Church multiplied. Though he had been discreetly tolerant of the Patriote movement in 1837–8, he vigorously opposed the efforts of the Rouge leaders to introduce into Quebec the advanced democratic ideas which they had absorbed from French and American sources. He frowned upon their newspapers, *L'Avenir* and *Le Pays*, and upon their Institut Canadien, a literary and debating society which encouraged a freedom of speech and thought not at all to his taste, particularly at a time when the English Protestants of Montreal had launched a vigorous effort to win the French Canadians away from Catholicism. The Bishop's apocalyptic sense of "the dangers of the times in which we live, the dangers from the men among whom we live, and the dangers of the errors of the environment in which we live" was heightened by the papal *Syllabus of Errors* (1864), which led him to declare a war to the death upon the Rouges and all their works. He and his fervent disciples virtually destroyed the Rouges as a political party. But when he and Bishop Laflèche attempted to set up a Catholic party in 1871 within the Conservative party, which now seemed to them almost as badly tainted by the errors of the age, they precipitated a conflict between English and French, Protestant and Catholic, which racked not only Quebec but the whole young Dominion. It was in this era of the so-called "Holy War" in Quebec that Laurier made his political debut.

In his early days Laurier was a Rouge and in 1863 he was a member of a committee of the Institut Canadien which waited upon Bishop Bourget when that highly conservative prelate proposed to censor the Institut's library. Laurier became a vice-president of the Institut in 1865, retiring only when he left Montreal the following year. It would appear that he had acquired certain English notions of free speech and thought from his mixed education, and that he was not in sympathy with the zealous bishop's effort to enforce intellectual conformity. Considering the war to the death—and in the case of Joseph Guibord, beyond death—that subsequently developed in Montreal between Bishop Bourget and the Institut, it was probably fortunate for Laurier's career that the threat of tuberculosis drove him in 1867 from the city to the peaceful hills of the Eastern Townships. Finally settling in Arthabaska, he combined the practice of law with the editing of a Rouge newspaper, *Le Défricheur*, founded by Eric Dorion, the fiery younger brother of Antoine-Aimé Dorion. Frowned on by the clergy who made common cause with the Conservative party, the paper soon had to suspend publication.

Like most young French-Canadian lawyers, Laurier was as active in politics as in his profession. He was elected to the provincial legislature in 1871, and three years later to the House of Commons. Though he was soon considered for a cabinet post, he hesitated to accept office in the Mackenzie government because of the prospect of strife with the clergy. It was as a battle-scarred veteran of the campaign of Bishops Bourget and Laflèche and their ultramontane followers that Laurier spoke at Quebec in June 1877 on "Political Liberalism" (U. Barthe, *Wilfrid Laurier on the Platform* [Quebec, 1890], pp. 52–79). This notable address, which first made him a national figure, was an effort to clarify the confusion of religion and politics which at that time threatened the future of the ten-year old Confederation. It was an eloquent demonstration of how Laurier reconciled his political convictions, derived from Britain, with his French and Catholic heritage.

Laurier began by refuting the ultramontane contention that Liberalism was a heresy condemned by the Pope, and that a Catholic could not be a Liberal. He denied that English political liberalism was identical with the continental European Catholic liberalism condemned by Pope Pius IX in the *Syllabus of Errors* of 1864. He blamed the confusion prevalent about the question on the fact that Quebec studied the history of the Continent, where "the history of liberalism has been written in letters of blood," rather than that of England, "the classic land of liberty." Citing Macaulay's definitions of conservatism and liberalism, Laurier declared that both sides were theologically indifferent, capable of much good as well as of much evil. He made a moving declaration of his own liberalism:

I am one of those who think that everywhere, in human matters, there are abuses to be remedied, new horizons to be opened up, and new forces to be developed.

Moreover, Liberalism seems to me in all respects superior to the other principle. The principle of Liberalism is inherent in the very essence of our nature, in that desire for happiness with which we are all born into the world, which pursues us through life, and which is never completely gratified this side of the grave. Our souls are immortal, but our means are limited. We constantly gravitate towards an ideal which we never attain. We dream of good, but never attain the best. We reach only the goal we have proposed for ourselves, to discover new horizons opening up which we had not even suspected before. We rush toward them, and those horizons, explored in their turn, reveal to us others, which lead us ever further and further.

This condition of our nature is precisely what makes the greatness of man, for it condemns him irrevocably to movement, to progress: our means are limited but our nature is always perfectible, and we have the infinite for our arena. Thus there is always room for improvement of our condition, for the perfecting of our nature, and for the attainment of an easier life by a larger number. Here again is what in my eyes constitutes the superiority of Liberalism.

Laurier contrasted the history of England, where reform had been brought about without violence, with that of the Continent, where repression had produced social explosions. He cited the great English Liberals: Fox, O'Connell, Grey, Brougham, Russell, noting that many of them were aristocrats who sacrificed their own privileges for the good of the people. He quoted Macaulay's triumphant account of the passage of the Reform Bill, which had deprived the historian of his seat for a rotten borough. Laurier maintained that such were the models, the principles, the party of the Canadian Liberals; they were not to be identified with the so-called liberals of France, Italy and Germany, who to his mind were not liberals but revolutionaries: "in their principles they are so extreme that they aim at nothing less than the destruction of modern society. With these men we have nothing in common; but it is the tactic of our adversaries always to assimilate us to them."

Turning from his defence of the Liberal party to an attack on the Quebec ultramontane Conservatives, Laurier accused them "of judging the political situation of the country not according to what is happening in it, but according to what is happening in France . . . of wanting to introduce here ideas which are impossible of application in our state of society." His main charge against the ultramontanes was that they were working hard and all too well "to degrade religion to the simple proportions of a political party." Laurier declared that he himself had "too much respect for the faith in which I was born ever to use it as the basis of a political organization." Then he went on to voice the first of his many warnings against parties organized on a religious or racial basis:

You wish to organize a Catholic party. But have you not considered that if you have the misfortune to succeed, you will draw down upon your country calamities of which it is impossible to see the consequences?

You wish or organize all Catholics into one party without other bond, without other basis than a common religion. But have you not reflected that by that very fact you will organize the Protestant population as a single party, and that then, instead of the peace and harmony now prevailing between the different elements of the Canadian population, you will throw open the doors to war, a religious war, the most terrible of all wars?

Like Elgin, like Cartier, like Macdonald, like all Canadian leaders who have profoundly understood the problem of governing Canada, Laurier knew that Canadian parties must be inclusive rather than exclusive, that French and English, Catholic and Protestant, must collaborate if the peaceful and prosperous union in diversity envisaged at Confederation was to be attained.

Because political life in Quebec in the 1870's had become what was aptly called a Holy War, with the conflict of clericalism and anti-clericalism, of gallicanism and ultramontanism, because his party was threatened with extinction in Quebec by clerical intervention in politics in behalf of the Conservatives, Laurier defined his position on the question of the day. He maintained that there was not one Canadian Liberal who wanted to prevent the clergy from taking part in politics, if they wanted to do so: "Let the priest speak and preach as he thinks best, and no Canadian Liberal will dispute that right." The priest had the same right as every citizen to take part in the business of government; not only to express his own opinion, but to attempt to influence the opinion of others. But Laurier added:

I am here to speak my whole mind, and I may add that I am far from finding opportune the intervention of the clergy in the domain of politics as it has been exercised for some years. On the contrary I believe that from the standpoint of the respect due to his character, the priest has everything to lose by meddling in the ordinary questions of politics; still his right to do so is indisputable, and if he thinks it proper to use that right, our duty as Liberals is to guarantee it to him against all denial.

Laurier pointed out that this right was, however, not unlimited, if it interfered with the voter's independence, with his right to cast his ballot freely as he deemed best. He gave a careful analysis of the electoral laws:

The law watches with so jealous an eye over the free expression of the elector's opinion as it really is that, if in a constituency the opinion expressed by a single elector is not his real opinion, but an opinion forced upon him by fear, fraud, or corruption, the election must be annulled.

It is therefore perfectly legitimate to alter the elector's opinion by argument and every other means of persuasion, but never by intimidation. As a matter of fact, persuasion changes the elector's conviction, intimidation does not. When by persuasion you have changed the elector's opinion, then the opinion he expresses is his own; but when by terror you force him to vote, the opinion he expresses is yours; remove the cause of his fear and he will then express another opinion, which is his own.

Now it will be understood that if the opinion expressed by the majority of the electors is not their real opinion, but an opinion forced from them by fraud, threats, or corruption, the constitution is violated, and you do not have government of the majority but government of a minority.

To Laurier it seemed that if the real will of the people were not expressed, responsible government became an empty and meaningless term. He feared that the inevitable result of such violation of the constitution, in Canada as elsewhere, would be social explosion, violence and ruin.

To his opponent's claim that the clergy had a right to dictate to the people its duties, Laurier answered:

We are here under the government of the Queen of England, under the authority of a constitution which was granted to us as an act of justice, and if the exercise of the rights which you claim is to have for effect the impeding of the constitution, and our exposure to all the consequences of such an act, then the clergy themselves would not want it.

He had a final word for the clergy themselves:

I am not one of those who parade themselves as friends and champions of the clergy. I say this, however: like most of my young fellow countrymen, I have been reared among priests and among young men who have become priests. I flatter myself that I have some sincere friends among them, and to them I can and do say: see if there is under the sun a country where the Catholic Church is freer or more privileged than here. Why then should you, by claiming rights incompatible with our state of society, expose this country to agitations of which it is impossible to foresee the consequences?

Laurier closed this forthright demarcation of the rights of the clergy and of the citizen with an eloquent tribute to the free British institutions which had enabled the French Canadians to remain French and Catholic under the British flag, whose sole defence now rested "in the gratitude which we owe it for our freedom and for the security we have found under its folds."

Laurier's courageous protest against the excesses of the ultramontanes—a protest which did much to relieve the tension which had been building up between English and French, Protestant and Catholic—soon found support in the highest ecclesiastical quarters, as well as in the courts. Bishop Conroy, the apostolic delegate who had been sent to Canada that spring to settle the vexed question of clerical intervention in politics, caused the hierarchy to issue a joint pastoral letter on the subject early in October. This pronouncement made the same distinction as Laurier had done between political and Catholic liberalism, and declared that the Holy See's strictures against Catholic liberalism were not to be applied to any particular political party. Members of the clergy were reminded in an accompanying circular letter that they were forbidden "to teach from the pulpit or elsewhere that it is a sin to vote for any particular candidate or party. . . . You are never to give your personal opinion from the pulpit."

This pronouncement did not come in time to prevent Laurier from being defeated in the Drummond-Arthabaska by-election made necessary by his entry into the federal cabinet. His opponents used all the old ultramontane charges against the Liberals. Dr. Skelton's well-worn tale is still the best account of the state of mind of the rural voter in those days. (*Life and Letters of Sir Wilfrid Laurier* [New York, 1922], I, 212–13.) One confused habitant told his *curé*: "I cannot vote for Mr. Laurier, for you tell me that if I vote for a Liberal, I shall be damned. I cannot vote for Mr. Bourbeau, for you tell me that if I do not follow my conscience, I shall be damned. I cannot vote for neither, for you tell me that if I do not vote at all, I shall be damned. Since I must be damned anyway, I'll be damned for doing what I like. I am going to vote for Mr. Laurier." Though a majority of the voters did not follow this course in Drummond-Arthabaska in October, Laurier did receive a small majority in Quebec East in November. His defeat in his own county left him with a certain bitterness against his opponents, who again made successful use of the same old tactics in defeating the Liberals in the federal elections of September 1878. The Liberals were to remain in opposition until 1896, but the power of the ultramontanes in Quebec was gradually broken by court decisions against them in cases of undue influence, and by the fact that each time Rome was appealed to, the decision went against them. It was difficult to be more Catholic than the Pope, and the ultramontane dream in the 1870's of a Catholic party soon died.

But it was not many years before another threat to the English-French partnership arose. In 1885 the execution of Louis Riel aroused a great storm of indignation in Quebec, and resulted in an effort to form a single French-Canadian party. Though at the mass meeting of protest held in Montreal six days after Riel's death Laurier had declared: "Had I been born on the banks of the Saskatchewan, I would myself have shouldered a musket" (Skelton, I, 314) he soon withdrew his support from Honoré Mercier's attempt to unite the French Canadians in a single racial party. To Laurier this seemed as fatally unwise for his people as the attempt to form a Catholic party, since it inevitably would unite the English Canadians against them. The violence of the Ontario reaction against the Quebec agitation was alarming. On November 25, a few days after the Montreal mass meeting, the *Toronto Mail* warned Mercier that "if the cabinet should fall as a result of the intrigues of French influence, if such is the fruit of Mr. Mercier's program, then, as Britons, we believe that the Conquest will have to be fought over again. Lower Canada may depend upon it, there will be no new treaty of 1763. The victors will not capitulate next time." (Skelton, I, 316.) The tension continued to grow after Parliament met in February 1886. In a speech in the House on March 16 Laurier denied Ontario charges that the French Canadians wished to suspend the operation of the law when a compatriot was involved. While he censured the Macdonald government for its long neglect of the grievances of the Métis, he renounced Mercier's answer to the question which had divided Canada:

It would be simply suicidal for the French Canadians to form a party by themselves. Why, so soon as the French Canadians, who are in a minority in this House and this country, were to organize as a political party, they would compel the majority to organize as a political party, and the result must be disastrous to themselves. We have only one way of organizing parties. This country must be governed, and can be governed, only on questions of policy and administration. [Barthe, p. 256.]

In accordance with this principle, Laurier attacked the government for the neglect which had fostered rebellion, and for the different treatment given the French and English rebellion prisoners. Inspired by the study he had made of Lincoln's career, Laurier urged the government to be guided by a spirit of mercy rather than one of revenge in dealing with the remaining prisoners. This was Laurier's first major speech in English. The Conservative *Montreal Star* did not hesitate to call him the "silver-tongued Laurier," while his own colleague Edward Blake referred to this speech as "the crowning proof of French domination," since by it Laurier had added the palm for parliamentary eloquence in English to his reputation as the best French orator in the House. To ease the tension between English and French which continued to grow, Laurier discussed the question in Toronto in December 1886, in the same terms he had used at Ottawa.

While Mercier went on to build his Parti National on Riel's grave, invoking the shadow of the gibbet of Regina at ninety political meetings, Laurier as the new federal Liberal leader became increasingly disturbed by the Quebec leader's tendency to exploit the emotions conjured up by such words as *national*, *Français* and *catholique*, rather than to use the reasoned arguments demanded by the basic political questions of policy and administration. Despite Mercier's promises to respect the rights of the English Protestant minority in Quebec, despite his professions of a desire to live in peace with all races and creeds, despite his promises to give justice to all, even to those who refused justice to the French Canadians, the English Canadians were alarmed by a provincial premier whose watchword was "national" in a racial sense, and who tended increasingly to act like the ruler of an independent state. Laurier took advantage of a St. Jean-Baptiste Day celebration at Quebec in 1889, when he appeared on the same platform with Mercier, to sound a different note than Mercier's call on that occasion for all French Canadians to cease their fratricidal strife and unite. He opposed his own inclusive Canadianism to Mercier's French Canadianism, his nationalism to Mercier's provincialism, with a moving eloquence equal to Mercier's:

We are French Canadians, but our country is not confined to the territory overshadowed by the citadel of Quebec; our country is Canada, it is the whole of what is covered by the British flag on the American continent, the fertile lands bordered by the Bay of Fundy, the St. Lawrence Valley, the Great Lakes region, the prairies of the West, the Rocky Mountains, the lands washed by the famous ocean whose breezes are said to be as sweet as the breezes of the Mediterranean. Our fellow-countrymen are not only those in whose veins runs the blood of France. They are all those, whatever their race or whatever their religion, whom the fortunes of war, the chances of fate, or their own choice have brought among us, and who acknowledge the sovereignty of the British Crown. . . . The first place in my heart is for those in whom runs the blood of my own veins. Yet I do not hesitate to say that the rights of my fellow-countrymen of different origins are as dear to me, as sacred to me, as the rights of my own race, and if it unfortunately happened that they were ever attacked, I would defend them with just as much energy and vigor as the rights of my own race. . . . What I claim for us is an equal share of the sun, of justice, of liberty; we have that share, and have it amply; and what we claim for ourselves we are anxious to grant to others. I do not want French Canadians to dominate over anyone, or anyone to dominate over them. Equal justice; equal rights. . . . Cannot we believe that in the supreme battle here on the Plains of Abraham, when the fate of arms turned against us, cannot we believe that it entered into the designs of Providence that the two races, enemies up to that time, should henceforth live in peace and harmony? Such was the inspiring cause of Confederation. [Barthe, pp. 527–8.]

Some might dismiss this as mere rhetoric. Those inclined to do so should note that Laurier used the same language in Ontario as in Quebec. He spoke temperately against the O'Brien resolution for disallowance of Mercier's Jesuit Estates Act in the House in March, and in Toronto in September. His moderate words, based upon an understanding of both the English and the French mentalities, helped to relieve the tendencies to racial division inherent in Mercier's movement and in that of the Equal Rights Association in Ontario. It is not belittling his course to observe that it also helped to knit the Liberal party together; here rather is a measure of his effectiveness in preaching a tolerant attitude when intolerance was running high.

Laurier's talent for conciliation was again displayed in the Manitoba school question, which eventually brought about the downfall of the Conservative régime in Ottawa. The question arose in 1890 when the Manitoba government, urged on by Dalton McCarthy and the Equal Rights Association's crusade against the French language and Catholic schools, abolished separate schools in favour of a single non-denominational system. Sir John A. Macdonald temporized by advising an appeal to the courts rather than a demand for disallowance or remedial legislation by the federal government. A test case was carried to the Judicial Committee of the Privy Council, which ruled that the provincial law was valid. The federal government then referred the question of its right to intervene to the courts, and the Privy Council ruled that it could take action. At last, in 1896, the Conservative government, headed by an ex-Grand Master of the Orange Order, reluctantly introduced a remedial bill, after the province had refused to obey an order in council requiring it to restore the rights of the French Catholic minority. Taking his stand on the grounds of provincial rights, Laurier opposed the remedial bill, while promising to win better terms for the minority. He resisted the intense pressure put upon him by the hierarchy to support the government measure, with a statement of principle on March 3, 1896, which reassured his English Protestant followers:

I am here the acknowledged leader of a great party, composed of Roman Catholics and Protestants as well, as Protestants must be in the majority in every party in Canada. Am I to be told, occupying such a position, that I am to be dictated the course I am to take in this House, by reasons that can appeal to the consciences of my fellow Catholic members, but which do not appeal as well to the consciences of my Protestant colleagues? No, so long as I have a seat in this House, so long as I occupy the position I do now, whenever it shall become my duty to take a stand upon any question whatever, that stand I will take not upon grounds of Roman Catholicism, not upon grounds of Protestantism, but upon grounds which can appeal to the consciences of all men, irrespective of their particular faith, upon grounds which can be occupied by all men who love justice, freedom, and toleration. [Skelton, I, 475.]

Laurier moved the six months' hoist. While the government defeated that motion, it was unable to carry the bill because of a filibuster by rebellious Conservatives. The question was carried over into the elections of June 1896.

Despite the solid opposition of the hierarchy, which issued a pastoral letter in May pronouncing the school question a religious one and directing all Catholics to vote only for supporters of the remedial bill, Laurier swept Quebec. French Canada, given the choice of following the bishops' instructions or electing a French-Canadian prime minister, supported the Liberals by more than three to one. As soon as Laurier took office, he at once began efforts to settle the school question. Negotiations between Ottawa and Winnipeg were made easier by the fact that the Liberals held power in both capitals, and that Laurier was pledged to the sunny ways of conciliation rather than to coercion. The Laurier-Greenway Agreement—actually negotiated by Israel Tarte and Clifford Sifton—was approved by moderates when it was announced in November, although it was condemned by both the Manitoba Orangemen and the Catholic bishops. In the face of continuing bitter clerical opposition in Quebec Laurier gave this advice to the young Liberals of Montreal in December:

Let me give you a word of good counsel. During your career you will have to suffer many things which will appear to you as supreme injustices. Let me say to you that you should never let your religious convictions be affected by the acts of men. Your convictions are immortal. Their foundation is eternal. Let your convictions be always calm, serene, and superior to the inevitable trials of life. Show to the world that Catholicism is compatible with the exercise of liberty in its highest sense; show that the Catholics of this country will render to God what is God's, to Caesar what is Caesar's.

Thus Laurier restrained the anti-clericalism of the inveterate Rouges, who wanted a war to the death with the hierarchy, and

101

yet encouraged his intimidated followers. Meanwhile he sent envoys to Rome. Mgr Merry del Val's resulting mission to Canada halted the renewal of the Holy War, and Pope Leo XIII's encyclical *Affari vos* of December 1897 put an end to the conflicts of Church and State which had troubled Laurier's early career.

I have chosen to devote so much time to this less known early phase of Laurier's career because here, to my mind, lies the evidence of Laurier's natural bent for conciliation of the two main cultural traditions of Canada, for working out a middle path between extremes which could be followed by all men of good-will, whether English or French, Protestant or Catholic, in a dual political society which was soon to become a pluralistic one. After he became prime minister, circumstances forced him, as they force any prime minister who is to survive, to the reconciliation of different groups, interests and opinions. But in his early days, as a private member, as a minor figure in the cabinet, as the rather insecure leader of a weak opposition, he developed a political philosophy and acted in accordance with the pledge he had made as a young man entering upon life.

Laurier did not diverge from this pattern in the fifteen years of his prime ministership, but rather developed his talent for the reconciliation of the differences of English and French Canadians in the interest of the development of the country as a whole. In the South African War, at the successive colonial and imperial conferences, he followed a policy which cannot be dismissed merely as "fifteen years of saying 'no,' " as Dafoe put it (p. 64). It was rather a delicate balancing of the imperialist and nationalist pressures in Canadian public life, in the light of Canada's future status as he defined it in 1908 at the Quebec Tercentenary: "We are reaching the day when our parliament will claim co-equal rights with the British Parliament, and when the only ties binding us together will be a common flag and a common Crown" (Skelton, II, 345). He clearly anticipated Canada's full nationhood, which one of his imperialist opponents of this period, Sir Robert Borden, later did so much to achieve by following much the same course as Laurier in the imperial relationship.

In the end Laurier's government fell before the onslaught of an uneasy alliance between his extreme nationalist and extreme imperialist opponents, made on one of the economic issues with which Laurier never really felt at home. He was quite well aware of the reasons for his defeat, as a 1911 campaign speech at St. Johns, Quebec, indicates:

I am branded in Quebec as a traitor to the French, and in Ontario as a traitor to the English. In Quebec I am branded as a Jingo, and in Ontario as a separatist. In Quebec I am attacked as an imperialist, and in Ontario as an anti-imperialist. I am neither. I am a Canadian. Canada has been the inspiration of my life. I have had before me as a pillar of fire by night and pillar of cloud by day a policy of true Canadianism, of moderation, of conciliation. I have followed it consistently since 1896, and I now appeal with confidence to the whole Canadian people to uphold me in this policy of sound Canadianism which makes for the greatness of our country and of the Empire. [Skelton, II, 380.]

His confidence was misplaced. The passions of both nationalists and imperialists had been whipped too high by leaders not as well balanced as Laurier, and the nation had become bitterly divided. The era of sunny ways was over.

Yet as leader of the opposition from 1911 until his death in 1919 Laurier remained faithful to his principles, displaying a high sense of responsibility under increasingly difficult circumstances as the rift between the races, which he had striven to heal, widened once more over the Ontario school question and the conscription issue. He gravely weakened his failing health by vigorous efforts to support the recruiting effort, and to moderate the Quebec nationalists' disregard for public opinion outside Quebec. Undaunted by the tragic divisions of the times between English and French, he summed up his philosophy in a speech at London, Ontario, in November 1917:

As for you who stand today on the threshold of life, with a long horizon open before you for a long career of usefulness to your native land, if you will permit me, after a long life, I shall remind you that already many problems rise before you: problems of race division, problems of creed differences, problems of economic conflict, problems of national duty and national aspiration. Let me tell you that for the solution of these problems you have a safe guide, an unfailing light, if you remember that faith is better than doubt and love is better than hate.

Banish doubt and hate from your life. Let your souls be ever open to the promptings of faith and the gentle influence of brotherly love. Be adamant against the haughty, be gentle and kind to the weak. Let your aim and purpose, in good report or ill, in victory or defeat, be so to live, so to strive, so to serve, as to do your part to raise ever higher the standard of life and living. [Skelton, II, 544–5.]

This is not precisely the conventional philosophy of a politician. It was the philosophy of a statesman. The fact that Laurier lived by it is best witnessed by the tributes paid to him after his death by friend and foe alike. One friend spoke of him as "the best man I have ever known. His instinctive honour, his kindliness and forgetfulness of self, that shining out of nobility and distinction which men call magnetism, made every man who entered his presence a better man for it." (Skelton, II, 558.) It was these personal qualities, arising from a philosophy held consistently from youth to age, which gave Laurier such a hold on the hearts of Canadians, regardless of their background. He first took a major role in public life when a young Canada was gravely divided, and he died when a much greater Canada was once more gravely divided. His lifework was a major contribution to "the conciliation, harmony, and concord among the different elements of this country," and one which was to inspire other men to carry on his work, and to give them heart for a task that is never wholly done.

FREDERICK PHILIP GROVE

One morning in December 1912, the deputy minister of education at Winnipeg found a stranger waiting to see him. The stranger was dressed in overalls, and he apologized for it, but the deputy minister said that he had in years gone by done manual labour himself, and overalls held no terror for him. The visitor, who was about forty years old, introduced himself as F. P. Grove. He was, he said, a European, with about twenty years' residence in North America. For a long time he had lived the life of a nomadic farm hand, working the harvest fields from Texas up to Manitoba, and "holing up" for the winter on the edge of some Canadian town. Now he wanted to try his hand at teaching, and he believed that his early education and present talents qualified him for a job. In addition to other attainments, he was at home in French and German, and read Greek and Latin almost as easily as English. Was there an opening for him in Manitoba?

Manitoba was currently short of teachers, and the stranger's tale made an impression on the deputy minister. There were difficulties, of course. It was not the customary time of year to engage teachers; and the stranger was unable to offer any documentation for his European education, which had, in any event, ended two decades before. But the fact that Grove was quite at home in the German language scored a point; there was a vacancy in a small settlement of Mennonites, recent immigrants from the German districts of Russia. This was at Haskett, practically on the border of North Dakota. Would Grove like to go down there? The department would be willing to give him a permit, and to set an examination in the spring to measure his academic standing. Then, if he wished to qualify for a permanent certificate, he could take a short course at Normal School in the coming summer.

By 1912, at the time of the interview, Grove had come to a parting of the ways: he had made some ambitious plans for the use of the next decade or so, and he accepted the Haskett appointment, though it was really only a rural school, paying a modest $50 a month. But even that sum was more than a casual farm labourer could hope to earn in the winter months, and the deputy minister had virtually promised Grove the principalship of a high school the following autumn if all went well.

So far, this kind of incident could be duplicated hundreds of times in the story of the west. I should not be telling it if Grove had been an ordinary sort of man. Many a transient, many a prairie farmer with only a high-school education, turned to school teaching when times were hard and teachers scarce.

What manner of man was Frederick Philip Grove? Here is his own self-portrait, drawn in *A Search for America*, as he appeared when he arrived on this side of the Atlantic:

I was six feet three inches tall, with a waist-measure of twenty-six inches. Hands and feet were narrow and long; my shoulders had begun to stoop. My hair was exceedingly fair—of that ancestral Scandinavian fairness that makes me to this day appear a much younger man than I am. My eyes were blue, arched over by bushy, yellow brows, and set rather deeply in a long, narrow face with a somewhat receding chin.

At 40 or 41, Grove was utterly unknown. He could boast of no achievements, beyond a wide experience of wandering over much of the face of the earth. He had not yet published a single line of prose or poetry. If anything then marked him out from his fellow immigrants, pioneering in central North America, it was an unusually rich background of reading and travel; and, more consequential, a passionate determination to write great literature before he died.

He had entertained this burning zeal to write immortal works for a long time, and he carted along, as he moved from place to place, a dozen or so parcels containing manuscripts. These were all written in neat copperplate, and on both sides of the paper. All of them had already been out on numerous trips to publishers but not one of them had interested an editor sufficiently to move him to write even a few lines of acknowledgment. Grove was mystified and frustrated by this, but it had not killed off his determination to write. When he went into the deputy minister's office at Winnipeg, he was still groping for an answer to a problem which has baffled more than one aspiring author: how to attempt serious literature without meantime starving to death.

Grove had read his Henry David Thoreau to good purpose. One way to become rich was by making his wants few. Grove believed that in a tiny self-constructed shack by some Manitoba stream, he could subsist indefinitely on an income of $25 a month. Such a sum in turn could be assured by a capital investment of $5,000. The catch was, he did not possess such a fund: he had only his harvest earnings of 1912, which came to $250. But if the salaries paid by the Manitoba department of education were as good as reported, he believed he could soon earn his independence. After a term at Haskett, he would move up to a high school, he would keep down costs, and save a thousand or so a year; so that by 1917, say, he would have accumulated enough capital to serve his life purpose. By then he would be getting on, he would be 45 or 46, but perhaps that would still give him time to become a great author. This dream suffered the fate of many similar dreams.

Grove became thoroughly absorbed in teaching. He was conscientious, and spent all his spare time and energy in teaching evening classes, which were his own idea. In a few weeks, he was offered the principalship of Winkler school, a few miles north. Here again he found an opportunity to serve far beyond his obligations. He organized classes up to senior matriculation level, spent all his surplus income to buy science apparatus which the board refused to supply, and equipped on credit a manual training shop, to cope with a threat of juvenile delinquency. By the end of two years, so far from moving towards financial independence, he was several hundred dollars in debt.

Then, in 1914, came what Grove calls in his autobiography "the decisive event," which was to close one phase of his life and to give the next a direction he had never contemplated. The young primary teacher at Winkler was a Miss Catherine Wiens, whose ability was exceptional, and whose classroom work filled the principal with admiration. This admiration and respect—which was shared—grew into friendship, and friendship deepened into romance. Grove visited her parents near Gull Lake, Saskatchewan, in the following summer vacation, and they were married at Swift Current on August 2, 1914. A year later a daughter was born, and christened Phyllis May.

It now seemed that Grove was committed to a career of teaching. For the moment, authorship was set aside. In the autumn of 1915, he went to Virden as master of mathematics, at $1,400 a year. That winter, however, he was stricken by an attack of pneumonia and he nearly died. He lost much time at school, and eventually resigned. In the fall of 1916, he found a new post as principal of the high school at Gladstone, northwest of Portage la Prairie.

Grove was now 45. His wife was still only dimly aware of his burning literary ambitions. His hopes of economic independence and the leisure to write great books had faded. The expenses at Winkler, the doctors' bills at Virden and the modest cost of furnishing their Virden home had run the Groves into heavy debt. His wife had ceased teaching when the baby was born. Not that they were unhappy: he was passionately devoted to his wife and the growing child. But the fatal urge to write would not be choked down. At Gladstone he found he had no evening work, and he got back at his books and manuscripts. One evening that winter, Grove read over to his wife a paragraph he had written years before. Her reaction was swift and decisive: "A man who can write like that," she said, "should not waste his time teaching."

When spring came, the old cruel urge to write revived in great power. The Groves debated the problem. Was it not still possible to accumulate a financial reserve, and thus permit him to take some time off for writing? To make a long story short, the Groves spent the next two years in an heroic effort to accumulate some capital. Mrs. Grove took the child and went back to teaching in a rural school north of Gladstone, while he taught a summer school for two months nearby. Then he returned to Gladstone school for the fall and winter of 1917–18, while she continued teaching in the bush country, thirty-five miles to the north. He was determined to spend every weekend with his family; and he did so, even in the vilest weather. These weekend drives became the material for his first published book, *Over Prairie Trails.* The following summer he taught summer school again: he was teaching around the year. They began to save a few dollars with which to purchase future leisure. So far the plan was working well.

And something thrilling happened during those two years spent a few miles north of Gladstone, in the bush-country which fringes the parkland and the treeless prairie—something of far greater importance than any improvement in their financial status. Odd as it may seem, Grove found up there an environment which exhilarated him, one which "clicked in his mind"—as he puts it—as the landscape of some of his most powerful fictional characters. In great excitement, as he explored the trails through the newly settled homestead country in the virgin bush, he had a feeling that he had found his North American home at last, after a quarter of a century of restless seeking. The very desolation of the country stirred him to the depths. It touched, he said, the innermost chords of his soul: it was a revelation. And all at once it came to him that for him nothing whatever counted, if it interfered with his life work. Here, he felt profoundly, he could create again, he could write the works he was so sure were waiting to be born. His imagination began to create furiously the characters and plots of such novels as *Settlers of the Marsh* and *The Yoke of Life.* Those, he said afterwards, were the happiest years of his life.

But, as so often in Grove's story, fate was ready with another trick to play, just when his fortunes were mending. He was driving along one of the bush trails on the margin of a swamp one July evening, when a wild dog rushed out at his horse, leaped, and seized it by the nose, hanging on for a moment. The horse reared, lashed out with his feet, demolished the buggy, and compelled Grove to jump for his life into a ditch on the north side of the trail. As he did so, something snapped in his spine.

There was no immediate cause for alarm, but he was rudely shaken up and continued to suffer from sharp pains in his back.

The following day his legs suddenly crumpled up under him, and left him helpless for a time. He was 48, and as it turned out, he was never again to be completely free from the threat of invalidism. Every now and then during the years to come, he was to have a breakdown, accompanied by a sudden paralysis of his lower limbs.

This raised a dark cloud over the Groves' future livelihood. At any time now he might have to give up teaching, and Mrs. Grove's own teaching certificate had not yet been made permanent. It became vital for her to complete her professional training, and to obtain a lifetime certificate. She must go on to Winnipeg and attend Normal School, while he must earn as much as he could, injury or not. What about the golden-haired little girl, now four years old? Grove found a post at Eden Consolidated School, and set up a modest establishment with the little girl; Mrs. Grove proceeded to Normal School at Winnipeg, with the intention of coming back for a visit once a month. It was in many ways a trying period, the husband liable at any time to physical collapse, the wife a hundred miles away in the city, the child too young to attend school. The future seemed uncertain. Yet, curiously enough, it was under these unpropitious and even hostile circumstances that Grove sat down to write what is in some respects his finest work, *Over Prairie Trails*.

This creative moment is worth elaborating. After a month at Winnipeg, away from husband and child, Mrs. Grove, perhaps for the first and only time in their life together, completely lost heart. She wrote despondently to her husband and seemed about to give up the Normal School course. He acted promptly, borrowed on a government bond, wired money to her for a visit back to Eden for a long weekend. And then, while waiting for her to arrive, he was seized he says, with a sudden inspiration: "I sat down at my desk and, in a veritable fervour of creation, wrote down, in its practically final form, the first chapter of *Over Prairie Trails*." The creative mood persisted all winter. With the setting and circumstances as uncongenial as possible, he entered into what was perhaps the most productive literary period of his life. Between October of 1919 and June of 1920, indeed, he wrote or re-wrote the better part of four books.

Two incidents at about this time fanned Grove's ambition to

become a professional writer. About the middle of November 1919, a man came to Eden who had himself written and published books, and Grove made bold to ask his advice about the marketing of manuscripts. The man, not otherwise identified, asked to see a manuscript or two. Grove showed him the volumes of *A Search for America* and the newly completed copy of *Over Prairie Trails*. These were, of course, handwritten and on both sides of the paper. "No wonder," he told Grove, "that you've never been able to interest a publisher. Your books have never been read."

Grove promptly bought a typewriter in Winnipeg and set to work making six copies of his latest book. He mailed them out to the leading Canadian publishers. In January—the Groves had left Eden and moved to a rural school east of Selkirk—a momentous letter arrived from McClelland & Stewart. *Over Prairie Trails* was accepted for publication in the fall of 1920! Grove was now approaching his fiftieth year, but it did seem at last as though his lifelong ambition was beginning to bear fruit.

Grove was still an invalid from his recurrent back ailment: each morning his wife would help him to his desk, where he sat and wrote propped up by pillows, while she went off to her rural school to teach the immigrant Ukrainians and other country children at Ashfield School.

The tonic effect of an acceptance from a Canadian book publisher spurred Grove on to even greater efforts. He set to work, he says, with tremendous enthusiasm, and a few months of amazing fertility followed.

That was again a very happy summer for the Groves. His wife was engaged to teach again at Ashfield; his back was improving; the little girl was healthy and happy; he was about to become a published author.

These idyllic periods in Grove's life never lasted very long. In the late summer he wrote to Toronto to ask when the proof sheets of *Over Prairie Trails* were to be expected. The answer was a shocker. Economic conditions had forced McClelland & Stewart to postpone publication indefinitely. Grove was to consider himself free to offer the manuscript elsewhere. This was a severe blow. The manuscript had already been offered to every other likely publisher, and had been turned down. Grove suffered a relapse and had to take to his bed. For months he was carried around to doctors and specialists. Out of $950 earned by his wife teaching school in that term, over $600 was spent on doctors' bills.

"I myself was growing weary," wrote Grove. "I had been writing for thirty years; there was nothing to show for it except stacks of manuscripts encumbering my desk." For a time he surrendered himself to despondency. "I did not mind being poor," he said. "I did not mind remaining obscure. What I did mind was that all my past and present echoed away in a void, ineffectual, useless." That, I think, was the low ebb, the blackest moment of Grove's creative life.

II

There were more troubles—there were always troubles—but in the east a few streaks of light began to appear. His health, after a further breakdown, now began to mend. Eden school was advertising, in the spring of 1921, for both a principal and an entrance class teacher. The Groves applied for the two jobs and they were both accepted. They stayed there for a year, and then moved on to even better paid work at Rapid City, where Grove was principal of the high school and his wife held the same position in the public school. Their financial position rapidly improved. Even more important to Grove as a writer, the proofs of *Over Prairie Trails* finally arrived from Toronto, and in the fall of 1922 the book appeared in print.

The immediate sale was modest enough, though typical for the Canadian market, and the cash return was small. But the publication had far-reaching consequences of other kinds. Grove at last had found a small but appreciative general public, and he won the acclaim and literary friendship of a number of discerning critics in the university and publishing worlds.

Once more Grove was stimulated: the appearance of *Over Prairie Trails* drove him back to his fiction manuscript *Settlers of the Marsh*. That summer, during what was supposed to be a holiday camping by Lake Winnipeg, he had a brief return of creative excitement, and during it he finished a dramatic episode in *Settlers* which so far had baffled him. Unfortunately, these inspired periods of creation were drawing to a close. This was to be, he wrote, the last but one time that the miracle happened, by means of which the words transcended themselves and became entities of their own.

Then, the year after the publication of *Over Prairie Trails*, McClelland & Stewart brought out his second book of essays, *The Turn of the Year*. Some critics think this the better of the two, and, indeed, his most perfect book.

In 1923, at Rapid City, Grove went back to his last year of teaching. His decision to leave the classroom after eleven years was partly voluntary, because he now wished to devote his entire time to writing, partly forced upon him by what he calls an "ever-mounting tide" of deafness. He had lost all his hearing in one ear long before, as the consequence of boyhood illness; now he became increasingly hard of hearing in the hitherto sound ear. It was one more hardship in a life filled with misfortune.

There is a pen portrait of Grove at Rapid City which helps us to see him at this stage of his career. Kay Moreland Rowe of Brandon (writing in the *Manitoba Arts Review*, Spring, 1949), tells the story:

"What was Frederick Philip Grove like as a person?" we asked one of the townsmen; an alert old boy, bright blue of eye, and his tongue still heavy with a North England accent after fifty years in Western Canada.

"He was a dour kind of fellow . . . never much for talking. Always seemed to have his mind working inside itself. He wasn't what you'd ever call popular, neither! He wasn't affable, was never one to stop and pass the time of day. Like as not when he did talk, in that careful clipped kind of way, he'd say something pretty sharp . . . so sharp it cut, often. And he wouldn't join anything . . . hated meetings of any kind. I remember how he'd stand up to the school board. He didn't understand us, and we didn't understand him. He was always fighting for more things for the school; always wanting more science equipment, more books for the library. He said that books were food for the mind and just as important as beef and milk for growing bodies."

"Was he a good teacher?"

"Never was any better than Grove . . . unless it was Mrs. Grove. Anybody around here'll say that. He was a man of true learning. Learning and teaching and writing was all that interested him." . . .

"What did he look like?"

"First thing you'd notice about him was his height. He stood about

113

six-two and was always rake thin. He had sandy hair and while you wouldn't call him handsome . . . still . . . it was a face you'd never forget. It was a thinking face . . . with a high thin nose and a strong mouth, and eyes that never missed a thing even when he was doing algebra problems in his head."

The publication of his first two books brought Grove some literary esteem in Canada and a few dollars in royalties. It spurred on his efforts to get additional works ready for the press. *A Search for America*, which had been written and rewritten six times over a period of three decades, was declined by Macmillan. He put that aside, and abridged a three-volume work he had intended to call *Pioneers*. Under the title *Settlers of the Marsh*, that too went forward to Macmillan. But a letter came back almost by return post advising Grove that no book of the kind stood a chance in Canada.

At this stage, Grove badly lacked a publisher with faith and insight. For his next book, he found such a publisher in the person of Lorne Pierce. In the fall of 1924, Grove was invited to give a reading of his work at Winnipeg: Lorne Pierce was present. Pierce asked Grove after the lecture to let him see the manuscript of *Settlers of the Marsh*, and made an appointment to have breakfast with Grove next day. When they met, Pierce said: "I had a very bad night, owing to that confounded book of yours." He had started to read it after going to bed and had, Grove says, found it impossible to lay the book down before finishing it.

In the following summer it was published by George H. Doran Company in the United States and distributed in Canada by the Ryerson Press. The result was startling. In the press and on the air it was described as obscene; libraries banned it; Grove says that he was himself cut dead in the street, and that Lorne Pierce nearly lost his job over it. Grove felt the criticism keenly: it was a frank but certainly not a pornographic novel. Nor did such denunciation have the usual effect of boosting sales and royalties. In every way the author appeared to be the loser over its public reception.

But Grove refused to be dismayed. He continued to get manuscripts ready for submission to editors. In the fall of 1927, Graphic Publishers, Limited, of Ottawa brought out *A Search for*

America, thirty years and six rewrites after it was first composed. Grove had by now become tired of it, and tended to think poorly of it, but it proved to be the most popular and enduring of his stories.

The popularity of *A Search for America* helped the sale of his next novel, *Our Daily Bread*, which Macmillan brought out. And acceptance of the *Search* again stimulated his will to write. Once more, however, tragedy struck just when prospects were improving. In July 1927, the child that had been the darling of their hearts was suddenly taken from them. This was the cruellest thrust of all.

Graham Spry of Ottawa, then national secretary of the Association of Canadian Clubs, was one of those who read *A Search for America*, and recognized in it a new and fascinating voice of Canadian letters. Spry thought that Grove's views about the European immigrant finding a spiritual home in North America might well interest Canadian Club audiences, and he arranged several speaking tours. Spry, now agent general for the Saskatchewan government in Britain and Europe, jotted down for me some reminiscences of Grove as he appeared in 1928, from which I quote here:

F. P. G., as I first recall him, impressed by his height and quiet reserved dignity. Both his figure and his accent reflected his Scandinavian origins. He belonged, in fact, to the Vikings in type.

In conversation he was not very forthcoming and had to be nursed along if he was to commit himself to any views, but once started he was a fascinating conversationalist on the subject of literature in which he was deeply read, and about his own problem of assimilating himself to Canadian life.

His literary interests were almost exclusively in English literature and particularly the English novel and late nineteenth century poetry. In this respect he was essentially a Victorian in his knowledge. . . .

Despite his previous financial difficulties he had acquired a rather extraordinary morning coat and also on occasions affected a cane. He did not, however, manage a cane very well and it was an ornament which somewhat embarrassed him even in walking. I recall that his arrival at the Rideau Club with myself and Martin Burrell, in his strangely cut morning coat and with somewhat dragging cane, caused some enquiry among the members; but seated

115

around after lunch, once he got going, he quickly earned respect. . . .

Returning to his physical appearance, may I say that he had light rather than blond hair; he was not only tall but his arms seemed extraordinarily long. His shoulders were reasonably broad and he walked with a slight stoop. When speaking, however, he stood like a naval officer, rather rigidly, and then slowly began to use his arms and hands in gestures. I do not recall the color of his eyes but they were probably blue, for his whole appearance, as I said, confirmed his Scandinavian origins.

After the Canadian Club tours, the Groves moved to eastern Canada to live. Grove had been offered some employment with the Macmillan Company, but unfortunately this fell through. Then he had a chance to join Graphic Publishers of Ottawa as editor. This was a long jump in seventeen years from the life of itinerant farm labourer. It even seemed for a few months as though he might, most improbably, become well off. His royalties, for the only time in his life, were substantial, and the Graphic job paid, for a short time, at the rate of $6,000 a year which was a good salary in 1930. As editor of Graphic, Grove entertained some ambitious plans for Canadian letters. He projected a series of Canadian historical classics. He founded a small exclusive publishing house of his own, and began to accept manuscripts of high literary merit but low box-office appeal. Unfortunately, the Graphic venture was even then on the edge of bankruptcy. When Grove parted from it, two of the historical classics had been printed and his own Ariston Press had issued two titles. That was the end of both ventures. Grove was stranded once more.

And by now Canada was deep into the Great Depression. Grove's royalties plummeted to near zero. He toyed for awhile with the idea of migrating to England. Instead he bought a dairy farm near the town of Simcoe, to which he moved in 1931, with his wife and the baby boy, who had been born the year before.

Meantime *The Yoke of Life* had been published by Macmillan, but had drawn few readers and a poor press. *Fruits of the Earth* came out in England in 1933, and in Grove's words, fell flat. Grove continued to write. At first he tried unsuccessfully to complete and market *The Master of the Mill. Two Generations* was written and, failing to find a publisher, was privately printed in 1939. *The Mill* finally appeared in 1944. To complete the story of his published works here, I should add that his autobiography appeared in 1946, and what he called his Ant Book, *Consider Her Ways*, in the following year.

When he died there were several unpublished novels. Possible future volumes also include an edition of his poems, a collection of his short stories, and an anthology or reader.

But I must go back briefly to trace the story of his declining years. When the Simcoe dairy farm, which they had hoped would provide a good living, became more of a liability than an asset, it was Mrs. Grove who once again stepped into the breach and saved them from further privation. Even with the new baby, their farm house at Simcoe was large enough to provide living quarters for themselves and permit Mrs. Grove to open a private school. This she eventually developed with striking success, attracting students from a wide area of Canada and the United States.

In the meantime, the years of depression and approaching war took heavy toll. Grove was driven to try desperate measures, even to attempt "Whodunits," to manufacture juveniles, to write tracts for the times. Little or nothing came of these ventures. In 1942, when he was seventy-one, he went out to do day labour again, in a nearby canning factory. There, he says, he met another elderly man, down on his luck, picking up a few dollars from casual employment. Grove discovered that he was a graduate of Oxford. "How did you get here?" Grove asked him. "Drink," he replied. "And you?" "Literature," Grove replied. Often near despair, he kept doggedly on with his literary work, as long as his health allowed. But in April 1945, he suffered a stroke which made further writing impossible. He passed away on August 19, 1948, in his seventy-eighth year.

III

As we have seen, Grove in his lifetime tried many literary forms: the novel, the short story, the essay, the lyric, auto-biography, literary criticism, allegory—even the detective story and the juvenile. One of the pleasant surprises to any student of Grove is his excellence in some of the minor fields. Popular attention has been focused generally on Grove's longer fiction. His most perfect work, however, is almost certainly to be found in his nature essays, his short stories, his literary criticism and his

117

lyrics. His most perennially interesting work is to be found in his two books of autobiography. However, it is as a Canadian novelist that Grove is generally presented today, and for the remainder of this talk I shall confine myself mainly to that part of his work.

Grove passionately wanted to write a great novel or group of great novels; I think there is no doubt about that. He greatly admired the masters in this field: Turgenev, Conrad, Meredith, Hardy, Tolstoi. He envied Hamsun, Rolvaag, Thomas Mann and Galsworthy their contemporary successes. He realized that of all the literary art forms, the novel was the one currently in fashion, and the one which might win him a place among the immortals.

Possibly he guaranteed his own failure in advance by setting his sights impossibly high. "What is the measure of a writer's greatness?" William Faulkner was asked recently. "The splendour of failure," he replied. If Grove really wanted to be the Joseph Conrad or Thomas Hardy of Canada—and there is some evidence that he so aspired—it can be contended that defeat was ensured in advance.

He possessed, certainly, some of the qualities of a great literary artist. He had a thorough intellectual grasp of the nature of tragedy, as can be seen from his essays in *It Needs to be Said*. He possessed an unusually intimate acquaintance with the outstanding literary works of Europe. He was an acute student of nature. He was versed in anthropology and archaeology. His writing style was adequate. He confessed that when he was writing *Over Prairie Trails* he realized that he had at bottom no language peculiarly his own. Instead, he had half a dozen of them. But this, he was shrewd enough to see, was a disadvantage and even a misfortune. "I lacked," he said, "that *limitation* which is best for the profound penetration of the soul of a language." But such a limitation was not in my opinion the critical one in his ambition to write great novels. For that he needed one gift above all, the divine gift of being able to give his creations abundant life. Had he possessed that gift in high degree, any stiffness in his style would have been readily forgotten.

As it is, the occasional clumsiness of his expression is not a serious defect. He mastered the essentials of English grammar, and his essay style rose at times to grandeur. His vocabulary could be painfully precise, and did not often become elegant or notably felicitous. For a novelist perhaps his most serious lack was mastery of the vernacular. He had a very limited ear for the colloquial rhythms of common speech. Indeed, it may be that his hardness of hearing and the effect it had in making him something of a recluse robbed him of the opportunities of registering often and deeply the raw stuff out of which a fine novelist creates his conversations. Grove's dialogue, especially the speech attributed to the younger generation, is one of the weaker elements of his fictional technique. Above all, he lacked humour.

He was handicapped, too, I think, in failing to find in time friendly critics and editors who might have helped him greatly to attain virtuosity in literary style. He was essentially self-taught. When he did find a sympathetic editor in Lorne Pierce, he was fifty-three and it was too late. By then Grove, with a stubbornness which you may think showed his artistic integrity, refused to change a line or even a word of his script, unless his editor or publisher was adamant, and not always then. He would withdraw the manuscript rather than yield. On balance perhaps this was wise, and it certainly protected Grove against those publishers who might have urged him to compromise and popularize his work in the interests of sales. But any conscientious editor, reading Grove's published work, itches at times to make minor textual changes here and there, to remove irritating flaws in diction or sentence construction. To be completely fair, some of these were due to excessive haste in preparing manuscripts for the printers.

A more serious handicap for the novelist has been suggested by both Edward McCourt and Isabel Skelton. Was Grove passionately interested in the fate and welfare of mankind? He said himself that he loved nature more than man. Did he really love people well enough to understand them? His portrayal of certain types of humanity was superb, particularly old men, masterful and ruthless, and men in their senile decay. But when he tried to portray adolescents or young lovers he usually faltered. Mrs. Skelton, in an article in the *Dalhousie Review*, drew attention to a passage in one of Grove's literary essays: "I abominate," he wrote—and this is strong language from him—"the common love-story—the story of pre-nuptial love—almost as violently as

119

I abhor the gramophone, the telephone or the radio. In life, both young men and young maids are peculiarly uninteresting at a time when they see each other as they are not."

Again, I think it was most unlucky that Grove did not receive some encouragement in his fiction while he was still a young man. It was not until he was fifty-four that his first novel was published. Most of the world's great novelists have been about ready to sign off at that age. He himself says that the last but one burst of miraculous creativeness had occurred a few months before. Who knows what work he might have done in the novel if he had won success twenty years earlier, before his deafness had advanced, and while he still mingled with young people and caught the nuances and rhythms of their talk?

The idea that there is any connection between the age of a novelist and his prospects of worthy literary offspring may be challenged. I believe that if I had the time I could make out a strong case. At any rate it is demonstrable that at least 90 per cent of the novels the world regards as great were not only written but published by the time the writer reached the age of fifty-four, when Grove published his *first* novel. Moreover, I toss in for what it is worth an assertion of William Allen White, the famous editor of the *Emporia Gazette*, that "Fiction is a matter of glands." When one is no longer interested in sex, Mr. White contended, and when anger has been succeeded by mellowness, then it is time to quit writing fiction.

How different it might have been for Frederick Philip Grove, if when he submitted to publishers an early draft of *A Search for America* in the middle nineties, he had found a sympathetic editor of the calibre of Lorne Pierce or Hugh Eayrs. He might have become a published novelist thirty years before he did, and his whole career might have been profoundly affected for the better.

It is idle to speculate thus. What does matter is that despite all handicaps, despite ill health, his desolation at the untimely death of his daughter, the indifference of the reading public and other discouragements, he persevered. Using time that was largely won for him by the heroic assistance of his wife, he succeeded in writing and publishing no less than seven novels before his death. I propose now to look briefly at each of these in turn.

IV

Settlers of the Marsh—Grove's first novel, published in 1925 and with two editions—is set in the bushland north of the open wheat plains of Manitoba. Grove called it a "garbled extract" of what was intended to be a three-volume work called *Pioneers*. He thought highly of it: "Personally," he wrote, "I thought it a great book; personally, I loved it as a beautiful thing." But, he added, its publication became a public scandal. As I have reported, it was denounced as obscene. The book never had a chance as a trade proposition; what sale it had was surreptitious. In another place, Grove said that the publication of *Settlers of the Marsh* proved an unmitigated disaster. It is not true, however, as has been reported, that its publication made it impossible for him any longer to find a position as teacher in Manitoba. His increasing hardness of hearing had already terminated his teaching career. Desmond Pacey thinks that though this was in some ways Grove's most ambitious novel it was not, in an artistic sense, his most successful. George Herbert Clarke and Carleton Stanley thought highly of it. W. E. Collin rather surprisingly finds in the novel not so much a story of pioneers in rural Manitoba as a symbolic ritual tale harking back to pagan days. Niels Lindstedt, the central figure, is a peasant type of grail questor, says Collin, and Grove's mystery is really a medieval romance. Isabel Skelton has mixed feelings about it. I come from a recent re-reading of all of Grove's novels with the conviction that this is his most artistic achievement, deeply felt and on the whole most successfully realized.

A Search for America, first published in 1927, is a blend of autobiography and fiction; it is doubtful if we shall ever know how much is history and how much is romance. The most popular of all Grove's published works, it has run through several editions and is still selling in a school abridgement. It was the earliest in composition of all of his books, and the style is easier and more flexible, perhaps as a result. Perhaps it caught a bit more of his youthful liveliness and fertility of imagination. When it appeared, Fred Jacob, the Toronto critic, wrote: "Of all the Canadian books that I have read, it is the only one I should like to have written." Isabel Skelton seems to have liked this novel best of all.

It has a dramatic lifelike variety, she wrote, which does not pall. "It is a unique Pilgrim's Progress, partly autobiographical, partly allegoric, showing how the author's outlook upon life became changed by the encounters he had with all sorts and conditions of men in the United States and Canada." Carleton Stanley says he has a higher opinion of the book than the author of it had. Grove, indeed, thought it was artistically his weakest book. It is a masculine book. There is no love interest at all, and the few feminine figures in it are casual and shadowy.

Our Daily Bread was brought out by Macmillan in 1928 and sold very well for a Canadian novel: over 3,000 copies in the first year. The setting is in what Grove calls the land of the sunset; bare, naked prairie hills, sun-baked, rain-washed . . . the Saskatchewan terrain, say, between Moose Jaw and Swift Current. Grove would have preferred to call it *Lear of the Prairie*, had Turgenev not anticipated him. This gives some idea of the theme. It is the story of a pathetic old man and his indifferent, ungrateful children who go their own selfish ways. Pacey thought highly of it; writing in 1945 he said: "Better novels than this may some day be written in Canada, but I do not believe they have been written yet." George Herbert Clarke is critical of its organization, but thinks that the final chapters redeem the book, especially the concluding account of the "grimly masterful hero's old age and death." This is a view I can personally endorse. Isabel Skelton thinks that Grove found a congenial theme in the old man's decay, but she feels that the reader, like his children, has lost interest in him before the end. He lacks Lear's majesty, his endowment of heart and spirit is so meagre that his fate appears less than tragic, she contends. He is not a noble figure defeated by circumstance, but a selfish man betrayed by his own selfishness. Edward McCourt comes to a similar conclusion.

In *The Yoke of Life*, published by Macmillan in 1930, we are again in the bush country of *Settlers of the Marsh*. This novel met with a cool reception, both from critics and from the book buyers. Only 571 copies were sold in the first year of publication and virtually none thereafter. Lorne Pierce called it a Canadian *Jude the Obscure*—and a pale copy at that. McCourt thinks that the hero, having begun as a recognizable human being, ends up as a symbol. Mrs. Skelton feels that the novel begins with the best opening chapter in all of Grove's writings, but that the theme, which is pre-nuptial love, is so abhorrent to the author that all comes to grief. The foundation for the existence of the lovers, she says, has been evolved out of theories, and in no scene does the novel hold the reader as a page of life and truth. Desmond Pacey is kinder, though he too thinks of it as a failure, even if a magnificent failure. Carleton Stanley called it a great book when it appeared, and in spite of a chorus of disapproval, he stood by his guns. "I not only think so still," he said fifteen years after its publication, "I am more struck with its greatness, its eminence in tragic pathos, every time I re-read it."

For *Fruits of the Earth*, published in 1933 by J. M. Dent in England and Canada, I have been unable to obtain an accurate note on sales. Grove himself says that it, like *The Yoke of Life*, was a commercial failure, that it fell flat. I do not myself care very much for it, but others value it as an accurate picture of settlement and farm life in the flat lands of southern Manitoba. McCourt praises in it the accuracy and maturity of Grove's approach to agricultural life on the prairies. Pacey thinks that if the ending were stronger, this would be Grove's finest book and that even so, it is surpassed only by *Our Daily Bread*. Mrs. Skelton regrets that the author found no beauty, no grace, no laughter or tears in the farm life of Manitoba. She thinks this is written in the most pedestrian and unimaginative style of all his novels. Nor, she says, does this academic man understand the simple unsophisticated rural Manitoba community. However, Pacey finds more sheer speed in its movement than in any other of the novels, and George Herbert Clarke points out that it is the closest of all to the physical details and social problems of the prairie. Perhaps it is because I spent my own boyhood and early youth on a prairie farm that I am less generous in my praise of this particular book. The surface activity of such a farm is well described: I miss its soul and essence and the inward life of the pioneer settler.

Two Generations is a farm novel with an Ontario setting. It was written after Grove had purchased his dairy farm at Simcoe, and by then he was already in his sixties. He was unable to find a publisher, and at last printed it himself, after selling sufficient copies by subscription to cover most of the outlay. It is a less ambitious work than most, quieter and more mellow. Grove himself called it "a mere trifle," but it bears the marks of much devoted craftsmanship and careful editing. Critics have labelled it one of his "pleasant" books. Pacey does not think it possesses the importance of the prairie novels, but Dr. W. J. Alexander rated it as "incomparably the best thing" Grove had done. I find it easy and pleasant to read, but it does not move me much, and some of the episodes and more than a bit of the dialogue are quite unconvincing. The theme is a favourite with Grove, and appears to stem from his own relations with his father; it is, once more, the clash between a domineering father and his wilful offspring.

The Master of the Mill, the last of Grove's novels to be published to date, appeared in 1944. Macmillan's figures show very modest but persistent sales: 650 in the year of publication, 400 the following year, smaller numbers in subsequent years—33, for example, as late as 1955–6, ten years after publication. This is Grove's only experiment in depicting the industrial scene. The setting is a gigantic flour-milling industry at the head of the Great Lakes. Grove did all the research for it as early as 1928. In 1934 he accepted advance royalties against it from J. M. Dent and Sons, completing the manuscript in hope of spring publication in 1935. Dent's English reader called it "a book on the grand scale, a book that demands admiration for its scope and its courage in tackling big and contemporary themes," but he did not recommend publication, and the manuscript was returned to Grove. It rested on his shelves for nearly a decade and appeared first in a limited edition in 1944. It is one of the few Grove books still obtainable. Lorne Pierce did not care for it. He wrote, "Only in *The Master of the Mill* can he be said to have produced a failure. It is melodramatic and unreal. His determination to tell all results in his telling little." Pacey calls it a "powerful" novel, but does not consider it Grove's masterpiece. Dr. Clarke says that the value of this novel depends upon its ideas and upon a few dramatic episodes, but adds that the constant effort to fuse fiction with thesis and exposition and the frequent troublesome shiftings in point of view impair its validity and power as a work of art. Personally, I found it an interesting and powerful experiment which impresses even in its failure.

V

What is Grove's place in Canadian literature? This is a difficult question which I should prefer to leave unattempted, but perhaps cannot evade.

He was never a popular author, and his name is not widely familiar today. Only three of his seven novels sold enough copies to cover publishers' costs, only two are currently in print. Any one of Ralph Connor's early novels sold more copies than the total sales of all those of Grove. *Anne of Green Gables* sold more copies in 1909 than the cumulative sales of all Grove's novels in thirty years. It follows that Grove's novels as a whole were not profitable to him in a financial sense. He made a net profit from *Our Daily Bread*, and with better luck *A Search for America* might have continued to bring in some income for years. But at best, in his own estimation, his lifetime of creative writing did not bring him in as much as two cents an hour, though he applied himself to it with rare devotion and industry for nearly fifty years.

Grove hungered after popular approval, but he would not compromise his art to seek for it. When in later years even his small public of the twenties seemed to peter out, he stoutly declared that he would appeal to posterity: only the future could decide whether his work was to count for anything in this world. It made him laugh, he said, when a book-reviewer called a novel of his a classic. "Why doesn't he wait a few hundred years," he commented, "before using such a grandiloquent word?" Grove thought that the artist should always build his work as if it were meant to last through the centuries.

We cannot, of course, foresee what future generations of Canadians will think of Grove. We can, however, get some idea of his stature from the testimony of his contemporaries. I have quoted favourable comments from such diverse sources as Fred Jacob, Isabel Skelton, Desmond Pacey, W. E. Collin, Carleton Stanley, W. J. Alexander, E. A. McCourt, George Herbert Clarke and Lorne Pierce. Watson Kirkconnell, Barker Fairley and A. L. Phelps were his friends and admirers. A small man would not have attracted the attention of such a cluster of literary critics. He was awarded the Lorne Pierce Medal of the Royal Society of

Canada in 1934. His autobiography won the Governor-General's medal. Two universities recognized his achievement by the award of honorary degrees.

Indirect tribute of a high order was paid to him in 1948. A committee of eight judges, representing five cultural societies, was asked by UNESCO to compile a list of Canada's 100 best books. Each judge submitted an independent list of 100; when these were collated, the resulting list contained 350. Frederick Philip Grove was represented in the 350 by 9 books—six novels, two books of essays and his autobiography. No other Canadian author scored so high. This list of 350 was reduced to the requested 100. The smaller list included two of Grove's novels and one book of essays: more than any other Canadian writer except Charles G. D. Roberts who matched Grove for first place.

When he died, the *Canadian Forum* said of him: "Frederick Philip Grove was certainly the most serious of Canadian prose writers, and may well have been the most important one also. . . . His life is a pitiful record of frustration and heartbreak, combined with a dogged insistence on writing as he felt without compromise. He is perhaps our only example of an artist who made his whole life a drama of the artist's fight for survival in an indifferent society. Yet one cannot help wondering . . . how much of his frustration sprang out of an obscure but profound will to be frustrated."

It was Lorne Pierce, in the *Transactions* of the Royal Society of Canada, who succeeded best, I think, in presenting a balanced account of his greatness as well as his inadequacies. Pierce said that although Grove wrote two long books which had for their main theme his search for himself, he failed to understand his own world and his own times, much less understand himself. In Grove's work "there is no overwhelming belief in anything outside himself, any overmastering love, no ineffable name, and no sanctuary." Grove's tragic view of life, Pierce added, "did not so much derive from the Greeks as from the lack of some overmastering passion . . . some sublime faith." Pierce, who had long followed Grove's career with hope and sympathy, then went on to examine some of his difficulties with language. But he could not end the appraisal on a negative note. "In a day of slipshod work," he wrote, "when sentimentality took the place of honest feeling, and prejudice did service for thought, Grove stood out like a mountain peak because of his integrity. While he lived, and suffered, and slaved at his laborious composition, it was impossible for any conscientious Canadian writer to take the easy way out with his craft. He moved through life with great dignity under all circumstances, and raised the vocation of authorship in Canada to a new height."

"What then is tragic?" Frederick Philip Grove asked in one of his essays. "To have greatly tried and to have failed; to have greatly wished and to be denied." But like Prometheus, even in our failure we exult, because we have fought with courage against the odds of life. In his later years, it is true, Grove sometimes yielded to despair and even declared his life to be an abject failure. Indeed, he set out to write his autobiography with the avowed reason of explaining to somebody—to whom?—why, after such bright early promise he had accomplished so little. Somewhere, he quotes Schiller:

> Into the ocean, with a thousand masts the stripling sails,
> Subdued, on a salvaged skiff, into the haven drifts the greybeard.

But is such a deflating experience peculiar to Grove? I do not think that the pessimism of his last years was warranted.

Prophecy, wrote the late J. W. Dafoe, is the most gratuitous form of error. Even so, I would dare to predict that Grove's reputation will grow. Future generations of Canadians will wonder about the literary pioneers. Grove was the first serious exponent of realism in our fiction. He left behind him a few exquisite essays, a few penetrating pages of criticism, some powerful short stories, two fascinating books of autobiography and a group of moving lyrics. There was, perhaps, no flawless masterpiece among his seven novels, but in some of the fragmentary and truncated efforts there is more sheer power and vitality than in any of the polished minor successes of Canadian fiction. Time has a fashion of eroding the weaker materials away, and leaving the peaks glinting in the sun.

STEPHEN LEACOCK

The labours which I have undertaken in the preparation of this lecture must be described as prodigious. There is no other fitting word. There will be many of you who will remember that passage in the works of Stephen Leacock in which he describes a man in the process of preparing a lecture: for the greater part of one whole winter the approaching lecture obsesses him; night after night he shuts himself up in his study, and if anyone calls, his wife explains that the professor is busy preparing his paper. I beg you to take note that this man is described as a "professor." So much the better for him; lecturing is his business, and he is able to appear before the world ticketed as a professional wise man. I am, I believe, the only author in this series who is not engaged in academic work; I am no professor; I hold no card in the wise man's union. Judge, then, how much greater was my anxiety in the months which have passed than if I were a professor. I am to talk to you about Stephen Leacock, and I have not even a gown to cover my shameful insufficiency.

It is not that I am ill-prepared. If anything, I am over-prepared. I have read again a large part of Leacock's work—not his books on political economy or history, but his comic inventions and his literary criticism—and I have sought information about him both from printed accounts and from the recollections —confided to me by letter and in conversation—of people who knew him well. (At this point it may be as well to say that I found many people who claimed intimate acquaintance with "The Professor"—as they all called him—who manifestly had known him only in the most superficial sense, and who attributed to him opinions which were obviously their own. The myth-making faculty, and the tendency to use a famous man as a personal sounding-board, are both at work on the creation of a Leacock Apocrypha.) But I lack a critical theory—a novel point of view. When I began my preparation, I had some splendid ideas about Leacock, but deeper study of his work banished them. He was too big to be caught in the net of any of my theories. What I am able to offer you, therefore, is a group of opinions not in themselves particularly original, but which you may think interesting in their arrangement or their application to a humorist and a Canadian writer. We have a way in Canada of not taking our writers very seriously. I propose to take Leacock as seriously as possible—as seriously, for instance, as if he were a Frenchman or an Italian, and not a Canadian, some of whose personal friends or uncritical admirers may be reading this.

Let me begin by reminding you of some of the biographical details about him which are relevant to a critical discussion. He was born in the south of England, at Swanmoor in Hampshire on December 30, 1869—which was, he reminds us, exactly midway in the reign of Queen Victoria. The Leacock family had made a good deal of money in the Madeira wine trade, but at that time it was running short. In his unfinished autobiography he tells us that among his early memories were the graceful sailing-ships lying at anchor, and an old sailor who was a veteran of "the Great War"—which meant the wars against Napoleon. On both sides of his family he came of what is called "good stock"—undistinguished people, but of assured social position— gentry, indeed. I think it important to remember that Leacock came of small gentry stock, for in later life he seemed always to be hankering for the stability of their values, and at the same time rebelling against what he conceived to be the injustice of inherited privileges; it was one of the tensions which plagued him, and which made him a humorist. For humour—as opposed to the mere mechanical jokesmithing of television, and similar painfully contrived fun—is always a result of tension in the mind. (Something of the same tension was observable in his later revulsion against the classics, upon which, nevertheless, he continued to draw heavily—particularly in the writings of his last years.)

The family story was one common in the history of all the British dominions. Because there seemed little likelihood that Leacock's father would do well in England, it was assumed— on some curious principle of nineteenth-century British logic— that he must do well in Canada, and in 1876 he and his family took up residence on one of those God-forsaken farms which Canada provides especially for Englishmen who know nothing about farming. It was a few miles south of Lake Simcoe. Here Leacock remained from his sixth till his twelfth year. His mother, of whom he writes with affection, strove to maintain the family gentility, and when her sons had tried the local school, and quickly took on the habits and grammar of the local farmers, she engaged a tutor to educate them as she thought fitting. But when Leacock's father—of whom he writes without affection—succumbed to drink and failure, and ran away from his family, she sent her sons to Upper Canada College in Toronto. In time Stephen Leacock became head boy there, and showed a marked aptitude for academic work.

When his schooling was completed, he taught school himself, at first in country schools; then, in 1891, he returned to Upper Canada College as a junior master, at the salary of $700 a year, and remained there for eight years, during which time he was able to attend some classes at the University of Toronto and take a degree. He hated school-mastering. It would be easy at this point to say some agreeable things about the teaching profession, but I shall deny myself that luxury. Let us agree simply that teaching children is a fine profession for those who enjoy the company of children, and who are happiest among those whose minds are less well-stored than their own. Leacock was not a man of that stamp. It is significant that he greatly enjoyed his work as a university professor, and gave it up with regret.

I should like to repeat here a story told me by Professor Keith Hicks, of Trinity College, Toronto. When Leacock was a master at U.C.C., another junior master amused and annoyed the Common Room by his repeated complaints about his salary. At last he requested Leacock to draft a letter for him to the Board of Governors. When completed, it ran thus: "Gentlemen: Unless you can see your way clear to increasing my stipend immediately, I shall reluctantly be forced to"—and here the page was turned —"continue working for the same figure."

Leacock had been given a classical education at school, but he turned towards political science in his university work. In 1899, having borrowed some money for that purpose, he went to the University of Chicago, and took his degree as Doctor of Philosophy—that degree which, as he says, signifies that a man has been filled as full of knowledge as he can hold, and must henceforth slop over. In 1901 he joined the Department of Economics and Political Science at McGill, and in 1908 he was appointed professor of that subject, holding the Dow Chair until he was retired, much against his will, in 1936. He won a great reputation as a teacher.

Now here I must advance an opinion for which I take full responsibility, though it is not my own. It was usual to refer to Leacock during his lifetime as an economist, and some people generously extended his reputation as a great humorist into his academic life, and declared that he was a great economist. It is on the same principle that the public often assumes that a man who is a great money-maker must also be a profound student of public affairs or an infallible prophet of the future. But I have sought the opinions of several eminent Canadian economists, some of them former colleagues of his, and they are in agreement on this: Leacock was not really an economist at all. In many Canadian universities Economics and Political Science are combined in a single department, following a Scottish tradition which can no longer be defended. It was so at McGill in Leacock's day, though it is so no longer. Leacock was expected to give some lectures on economics, and he did so. He was an inspiring and indeed a brilliant teacher. But when Leacock wrote on economics he wrote—and I quote one of my informants—"some damn fool things." (Of course the best teacher is not necessarily the man who has the most profound understanding of his subject. Canadian educators have for some years been propagating the theory that a command of the technique of teaching is vastly more important than a knowledge of the subject to be taught. Indeed, we are sometimes led to feel that knowledge is a positive handicap to a teacher.) Again, Leacock has been described to me as "an untrained layman" in the realm of economics, though the man who said so said also that his economic efforts were graced by excellent common sense. Whether this means that a truly professional approach to economics cannot be reconciled with common sense is outside the scope of this essay.

But though apparently no economist, Leacock was a good political scientist—careful in study, sound in argument and wise in judgment. However, it appears that his most important book on this subject, *Elements of Political Science*, is now outdated. Again, I quote from a professional economist:

Though his economic writings ought never to have been written, they really are irrelevant to his academic career. He was a great teacher of the subjects he had mastered. He was an inspiration to all who came in contact with him. He was a thoroughly competent political scientist, though his greatness did not lie there. Yet he deserved his professional honours on professional grounds. He was not an economist and it is a great pity that in his declining years he wrote on economic subjects. I hope a sympathetic biographer will forget these latter works.

I have given a good deal of emphasis to this point, because I want to make it clear that Leacock's importance to Canada rests solely upon the body of his work as a humorist. Perhaps that seems self-evident to you. It did not seem so to him. He was proud of his writings on political science and economics. He appears to have been proud, also, of his books on Canadian history, though these are unoriginal in viewpoint, and do not seem to me to be written with much literary skill. He also had a good opinion of himself as a literary critic, and on his work in this field I may presume to speak with some degree of expert knowledge.

He possessed some of the qualities of a critic—some of the rarest gifts to be found in that ambiguous and over-valued occupation—for he was a great enjoyer of literature, and he had splendid flashes of insight. Because he was himself a creative artist of uncommon abilities, he understood the toil of creation and the temptations of the creative life better than the parasite-critic whose only writings are fastened, leech-like, upon the body of another man's work. But he was inexcusably careless about matters of fact and detail; in his book on Dickens it is astonishing to find that he has not even troubled to verify the names of some of Dickens' characters. And he was extreme in his judgments: when he says that Dickens' works "represent the highest reach of the world's imaginative literature," we must smile, because we know that Leacock had not read extremely widely in English, not to speak of other languages which deserve some consideration when such broad claims are being made. When he says that Shakespeare was a man of "far lesser genius" than Dickens, it simply means that Leacock had a very poor ear for poetry—a fact which he makes plain in several other books, by quoting second-rate and third-rate verse as if it were of the first order. His book on Dickens contains enough good material for a first-class long essay, but it is a poor book.

There is an odd element in the Dickens book which suggests a strong strain of Victorianism in Leacock. He writes at length and with indignation about Dickens' estrangement from his wife, and professes not to understand how it came about. Yet unless he depended on secondary sources to a degree which was most unscholarly, he must have examined Dickens' will, and he must have noticed that the first legacy named in it is to the woman who was Dickens' mistress. If he knew that, why did he not refer to it in his book? Is the clue in a remark which he makes in the book itself that "Charles Dickens is not yet history, to be mauled about like Charles the Second or Charlemagne"? Or was Leacock really deluded about Dickens, and wrote what he believed to be the truth when he said "In him was nothing of the philanderer, the Lothario, the Don Juan"? Whatever the truth of the matter, it is important that we should remember that Leacock's character was formed before the modern vogue for easy self-revelation came into being. If we are to seek the truth about him, we shall have to read between the lines in his work, for we shall not find what we are looking for plainly set forth. In so doing we must remember that reading between the lines of anybody's work is an exceedingly delicate and tentative business.

Leacock was a writer all of his adult life. But his real career as a writer did not begin until his fortieth year, when he gathered up some amusing pieces which he had written for papers and magazines, and published them at his own expense, for distribution at news-stands. A copy of this now extremely rare publication fell into the hands of John Lane, the English publisher, who made Leacock an offer, and that was how *Literary Lapses* came to be published in 1910. It was a success, and was followed in 1911 by another volume of reprinted pieces, *Nonsense Novels.* Of the fifty-seven books which Leacock wrote, altogether the majority, and those which now survive, were humorous works. He made a great deal of money out of them. Indeed, one biographical article says—I do not know on what foundation—that Leacock made as much as $50,000 in a good year from his books. This seems a very great deal of money, and I think it is probably much exaggerated. But it is a fact that he achieved affluence through his writing, and would have been a rich man if he had not had a passion for investing in the stock market. We might naturally assume that a professor of economics would be an unusually shrewd investor; we would be quite wrong in making any such assumption. The temples of Wall Street, St. Catherine Street and Bay Street are built on the bones of professors with infallible systems for making a million. But during the years after forty, Leacock was in easy circumstances, and several times in his autobiographical writings he refers to this fact with pride. Any author who has tried to make money by writing will know how completely and utterly such pride was justified.

Recognition of his undoubted genius as a humorist came first in England, and quickly spread to the United States. It came much later in Canada, and when it came it was not marked by an ungovernable enthusiasm. It would be possible to offer many explanations for that state of affairs, but they would be somewhat unkind, and I shall touch on them lightly. In Leacock's heyday, which may be roughly placed between 1920 and 1935, we were not sufficiently sure of ourselves in this country to realize that a humorist may be a serious literary artist, like the man who writes books in a more sober vein. Indeed, we still retain much of that unsophisticated approach to literature which assumes that what makes easy reading must have been easy writing. We undoubtedly owe much to the earnestness and seriousness of purpose which marked our pioneer ancestors, but we may surely recognize now that there was a negative side to that condition of mind; Canada was settled, in the main, by people with a lower middle-class outlook, and a respect, rather than an affectionate familiarity, for the things of the mind. Worthy and staunch though they were, there was also a grim dreariness and meagreness of intellect about them which has shaped and darkened our educational system and which casts a damp blanket over our national spirits to this day. We can laugh, but we are a little ashamed of doing so, and we think less of the man who has moved us to mirth. We retain a sour Caledonian conviction that a man who sees life in humorous terms is necessarily a trifler. Leacock's life offers more than one example of this. I am told by a Torontonian who is in a position to know that, immediately after the First Great War, when Canada was much exercised on the Total Abstinence question, Leacock appeared in Massey Hall to give a lecture, in a state which left no one in doubt as to where *his* sympathies lay in the argument. Toronto was scandalized and Gundy, Leacock's Canadian publisher, said that for three years after this appearance not one copy of a book of Leacock's was sold there. In Canada we may know little about literature, but we are great experts on questions of Respectability.

It would be wearisome to dwell at length on what was said about Leacock by Canadian critics. One characteristic example will be enough. In the article on "Literature" in the *Encyclopaedia of Canada*, we read that "He is a kindly critic of the foibles and absurdities of humanity. He has created no outstanding character, being content to show up, with his ridiculous verbiage and boisterous fooling, the nonsense of common people about him." The tone, you will observe, is faintly patronizing. Certainly we are given no hint that a great man was at work.

It would be unjust if I failed to mention three notable exceptions to this general cool appraisal of Leacock in Canada. B. K. Sandwell knew his worth, and gave him his due. Pelham Edgar appreciated what he was, and has pointed out with cogency what he failed to be. And in the volume on Leacock in the "Makers of Canadian Literature" series, which Peter McArthur wrote in 1923, there is a remarkable appraisal of Leacock's value and also a suggestion of his potentiality which reads now like prophecy. I shall not quote fully, but I shall offer you a capsule of what McArthur says: in his view Leacock was already, at that time, being victimized by publishers and a public who could not get enough of the "ridiculous verbiage and boisterous fooling" to which Dr. Lorne Pierce refers, and was not developing as a literary artist; McArthur points out that his power of pathos is great, and that it lies in his power to be a literary artist—a novelist—of great scope. "As matters stand he is one of the truest interpreters of American and Canadian life that we have had; but by giving free play to all his powers he may finally win recognition as a broad and sympathetic interpreter of life as a whole." That Leacock did not do so was his tragedy—and ours.

I have used the word tragedy, and I do not intend to retract it, but on the other hand I do not want to push it too hard. When a man fails to realize the finest that is in him, is it really a tragedy? When a potentially great comic writer fails to become a great novelist—such a novelist as Dickens or Mark Twain—we may certainly say that the literature of his country has sustained a heavy blow. If Leacock had developed into a genuine heavyweight novelist the course of Canadian literature during the past thirty years would have been very different. Peter McArthur thought he could do it in 1923; as we look back now over the whole body of his work we must agree with McArthur. There is in the best work of Leacock a quality of sympathetic understanding, of delicacy as well as strength of perception, which suggests something far beyond the range of the man who could, in cold blood, produce a book with the flat-footed title *Funny Pieces* which he did in 1936, when he was 67 and the time for great developments had gone by.

The notion of Stephen Leacock simply as a funny fellow, who loved all mankind and passed his life in an atmosphere of easy laughter, varied with plunges into economics, must go. The notion that "ridiculous verbiage and boisterous fooling" were his special gifts, must go. There are in his books too many hints at darker things, too many swift and unmistakable descents towards melancholy, for us to be satisfied with this clownish portrait any longer. He was a man of unusual maturity of outlook, whose temperament disposed him to comment on the world as a humorist; at the top of his form he was a humorist of distinguished gifts, with a range and brilliance not often equalled. But the humour, though deep in grain, was not the essence of the man's spirit. That essence lay in the uncompromisingly adult quality of his mind, and the penetration of his glance. These were qualities which, if circumstances had been slightly different—if he had not been a humorist—might still have made him a writer of great novels, or even of tragedies. Why was it not so?

Here I approach difficult ground. Not the least of my difficulties is that I am strongly conscious of how deeply Leacock himself disliked criticism of the kind which I am about to attempt—the criticism which tries to read between the lines, which tries to throw light into dark places, which wants to open cabinets the subject has chosen to keep locked. My excuse must be the old one: great men do not belong wholly to themselves; everything that can be found out about them is of interest; their motives and their weaknesses are probed by those resurrection-men of literature, the critics. They are mauled about like Charles the Second or Charlemagne.

Leacock was proud of his huge output as a writer. He had a farmer's or a Canadian's high estimate of industry for its own sake. All his life long he got up at five o'clock in the morning, to work. He declared proudly in *Who's Who* that he published at least one book every year from 1906 to 1936. That his work became mechanical and stale, and that there was sometimes an hysterically forced note in his fun was less to him than that he wrote a funny book every year. He made ferocious fun of industrialists in *Arcadian Adventures among the Idle Rich* and *Moonbeams from the Larger Lunacy*, but he was just as much under the compulsion to work, to produce, as they were. Why did he do it?

Frankly, I think he did it to make money. He had what we may call an addicted public, like P. G. Wodehouse. There were very large numbers of people who bought every book he wrote and who read and re-read them. Such people are not critical readers; they are attracted to a writer by something special in his work, and they want that special thing repeated, over and over again. To such readers nothing is more baffling than a writer who insists on trying something new, who experiments or improves. Recently Mr. J. B. Priestley made an irritable protest when in Canada about being associated always and forever with *The Good Companions*—his first big success. Any author who is more than a hack or a society clown knows precisely how Mr. Priestley felt. To be judged by what you have left behind—that is bitter indeed. Yet Leacock seems to have embraced his chains, and gloried in ploughing the same field over and over again. I have said that I think he did it for money.

And why not, you may ask. Certainly, why not? Authors like money as well as anyone else. But authors are occasionally—not invariably—artists as well, and there are supposed to be some things which they prize even beyond money. The time must have come in Leacock's life—when he reached the age of fifty—when he had enough money, we would say.

Ah, but that is the nub of it! *We* would say it, sitting at ease in our seats of judgment, surveying his life, but would *he* have said it? Have you ever known an instance of a man who tasted the bitterness of poverty in his youth who ever felt that he had enough money in his maturity? I have known only one such instance in all my experience of rich men and he is so extraordinary as to be considered almost insane by his wealthy friends. Leacock had the wretchedness of that pioneer farm in his bones to the end; he remembered his mother's struggles to keep the ship afloat on her private income of eighty dollars a month, when he was a school-boy. Sometimes, when he had grown old, he boasted of his affluence. But he never had enough money to set him free from the desire for more.

And that desire led him to accede to the urgencies of his publishers and of his faithful public to produce books in his familiar, well-worn vein until it was too late to do anything else. He wrote in his unfinished autobiography that poverty was one of the chief drawbacks to being a schoolteacher; he uses a phrase in this connection which sticks in the mind—he says that the teacher ought to be able to feel that he is "as good as anybody else," and he seems to associate this feeling principally with money. Scholarship, the respect paid to education (not that this has ever been a big factor in Canada), the pleasures of a well-stored mind—these things are as dross if a man has not enough money. Leacock, it seems to me, spent a great part of his life trying to show that he was "as good as anybody else." The trouble is, of course, that if you set out to prove that, and make money your standard, you have embraced a career of disappointment, for you will always find that, however much money you amass, there is somebody who has a little more, and who is therefore, by your own standard, better than you are. It is odd that an economist should have fallen into such a curious state of mind. Yet, when we read in the book on Dickens that "There is no man living who can overcome the prejudice of social disadvantages," we think of the genteel poverty of the farm on Lake Simcoe; we think of the poverty, not at all genteel, of student and schoolmastering days, and we can find it in our hearts to forgive much that was undertaken "to be as good as anybody."

I do not believe for an instant that a man of Leacock's stamp spent his life getting money simply in order to have. He wanted popularity, too. That solid audience, which bought every book, was very dear and reassuring to him. We know that he delighted, quite legitimately and rightly, in his popularity among his students. He was a man of many friendships, and apparently he could be a demanding and absorbing friend. Let me quote from a letter written to me by one who knew him:

He had an enormous gift for friendship. Almost a terrifying one, because he could consume a man. In one case, well known . . . he did. The man ceased to exist as an intellectual being after Stephen died. As a friend Stephen was too rich a diet, and too demanding for the frail. . . . I've mixed some metaphors there, but I hope my point comes through.

Leacock needed popularity, as Dickens needed it, not from simple vanity but because it was the very air on which he fed, the reassurance that he was truly the public figure he had so painstakingly built up.

Was Leacock aware that there was danger in his popularity, and in his yielding to popular demand that he repeat his effects? Yes, I think he was, for it is a strange characteristic of great men that they can anatomize the very ills which seem to be destroying them. When he wrote in his book on Dickens, "You encourage a comic man too much and he gets silly," and again that "Praise and appreciation, the very soil in which art best flourishes, may prompt too rank a growth," he certainly knew what was happening to himself. But in every man there are many men, and the underpaid young schoolmaster in Stephen Leacock, who did not feel that he was "as good as anybody else," needed that praise and that solid audience, and was not inclined to risk losing it by experiment—even if experiment meant artistic growth.

Did Leacock think of himself as an artist? Unquestionably he did. He may not have used that actual word, because it is a word which makes many people shy, but certainly he knew himself to be a man of extraordinary gifts as a writer, and he cultivated those gifts assiduously in the fashion he thought best. What is that if it is not being an artist? He took a step at which many an artist has baulked— he undertook to explain the secrets of his art in one of the most unhappy of his books—the one called *How to Write*. In it he attempts to guide the steps of the beginner, and it is not all bad—it was not possible for Leacock to write a book which was bad from start to finish. But the book is chiefly interesting for what it tells us about the writer—what he thought about himself and his work. In this book, by the way, his extraordinary talent for misquotation and misattribution reached its finest flights; it seems astonishing that his publishers would have allowed a book containing so many howlers to go forth under their imprint. Quite the most embarrassing chapters in it are the two in which he undertakes to tell his reader how to write humour.

Now Leacock could no more tell anybody how to write humour than Jove could tell them how to turn into a bull, or a swan, and for the same reason—it was his special gift, his godhead, not susceptible of analysis or explanation. Yet he could not resist giving advice on the subject, and he seized every opportunity to hold forth on the nature of humour; it was the only subject on which he was ever pompous or silly.

Only once, in the whole body of Leacock's work, have I found a passage about humour, or the writing of it, which is worthy of him. I determined when I undertook this study that I would not pad with quotations, but I hope that you will permit this one extended passage:

Once I might have taken my pen in hand to write about humour with the confident air of the acknowledged professional. But that time is past. Such claim as I had has been taken from me. In fact, I stand unmasked. An English reviewer writing in a literary journal, the very name of which is enough to put contradiction to sleep, has said of my writing, "What is there, after all, in Professor Leacock's humour but a rather ingenious mixture of hyperbole and myosis?" The man was right. How he stumbled upon this trade secret, I do not know. But I am willing to admit, since the truth is out, that it has been my custom in preparing an article of a humorous nature, to go down to the cellar and mix up half a gallon of myosis with a pint of hyperbole. If I want to give the article a decidedly literary character, I find it well to put in about half a pint of paresis. The whole thing is amazingly simple.

Now there we have the authentic voice of Leacock, the magician who could turn the leaden words of a critical jackass into the pure gold of his own delightful fun. But in *How to Write* we are saddened by the spectacle of the same magician, so eager to be popular with his audience that he is even willing to explain how his tricks are done. (His best advice on writing remains that pungent comment: "Writing is no trouble: you just jot down ideas as they occur to you. The jotting is simplicity itself—it is the occurring which is difficult.")

Only an artist could write like Leacock at his best. And only a man who thought of himself consciously as an artist would have undertaken to explain how he did it. And only a man who yearned for popularity would have thought it desirable or wise to do so.

I have stressed his desire for popularity because I want to call your attention now to the extraordinarily successful public personality which Leacock created for himself. There may be some among you who remember that personality—the strikingly masculine impression created by the big figure with the big head and the rough mop of grey hair; the rugged face alight with intelligence and merriment, the twinkling eyes and the infectious laugh, the deep voice, which he used as skilfully as a fine actor— for Leacock was a fine actor, and perhaps the finest that Canada has ever produced. Do you really suppose that there was no calculation in the impression which he gave, in his expensive, though rumpled clothes, his dress tie usually untied, and his great watch-chain fastened to his waistcoat with a safety-pin? He was a great man; he looked and behaved like a great man; and he knew that he was doing so. Please do not suppose that I say these things in reproach: on the contrary, I say them in admiration. I, for one, have no use for a great man who creeps and crawls about the earth trying to be smaller than his natural size, for fear of giving offence to little men. But great men of Leacock's stamp know very well what they are doing. When I say that he created

141

a public personality for himself I mean that he did so as naturally, and as inevitably, and at the same time as carefully as his great heroes and masters, Charles Dickens and Mark Twain.

The word which pursued Leacock on his lecture tours was "fun." It is a word which is a little out of favour at present, for this is not an age when fun is much understood or valued. In our day humour has become, as never before, a marketable commodity, created and sold by committees of industrious, ulcerous, clever but basically humourless men to the movies, the radio and television. We have this commercial humour, with its synthetic clangour of empty laughter from studio audiences. And we have brittle, egghead wit, so fast and wry and nervous that it is exhausting rather than refreshing in its effect. But of fun—fun in the sense that the Edwardians used the word—we have very little. Leacock was a master of fun. He convulsed his audiences by a flow of nonsense which seemed so wonderfully easy that nobody sought to analyse how it was created. In *My Discovery of England*, which I personally rank among his best books, he tells how he almost killed a man in an English audience with laughing. This account was only slightly exaggerated. People who went to Leacock's lectures laughed until they hurt themselves; they laughed until mildly disgraceful personal misfortunes befell them. And Leacock laughed with them. He delighted in their laughter, and he gloried in his own power to provoke it. There was nothing of the dry humorist or the pawky joker about him. His humour was plenteous and bountiful. If at times it suggested the sledge-hammer rather than the rapier, this was the negative side which cannot be dissociated from positive virtues. He was in the greatest tradition, not of wit, not of irony or sarcasm, but of the truest, deepest humour, the full and joyous recognition of the Comic Spirit at work in life.

This was the Leacock who was known to the public. Was there another? Of course there was, and anyone who reads his work with any degree of attention must be conscious, from time to time, that that other man is revealing himself. I myself was conscious of this duality long ago, when I had no thought of making any critical study of his work. The command of pathos of which Peter McArthur spoke is indeed great, but I think that there are times when the pathos and the melancholy enter his work unbidden.

And if we think of the matter seriously for even a few minutes, do we not see that it must be so?

It is not Nature's way to extend a man's range far beyond the common endowment in one direction, and to make no corresponding and balancing extension in another. Great gifts carry with them great burdens. The notion of the clown who amuses the crowd while his heart is breaking is a vulgar cliché—but like many a vulgar cliché it has become so because it is the fossilized remainder of a valid and universal observation. A man is not able to look deep into the heart of life and see the fun and the nonsense there, and be blind to everything else whatever. A man is not capable of being carried aloft on the most astonishing and gravity-defying flights of pure delight, without also plunging into the depths, the abysses of melancholy and suffering. Nature is mercilessly insistent on balance and her own kind of order in human personality. Because Stephen Leacock was uncommon in one direction, he had, of necessity, to be uncommon in another. Unusual sensitivity is not confined to one realm of feeling.

This is not a fancy theory which I have concocted to make myself seem wise. What I found in his work, I have been able to corroborate in his life. Again I quote from a letter from a man who knew him and whose powers of discernment are beyond the common:

You ask about the possibility of Stephen being a melancholy person. There can be no doubt about that. He had a melancholy nature, and he endured personal sorrows which preyed upon him. I felt a distinction between the Stephen Leacock I knew as a flesh and blood person and the strange, admired, distant author. The person I knew was a strange, moody, even melancholy man, sometimes defensive among his professional colleagues and definitely short-tempered. He was prickly, quick to take offence, insecure—so the modern jargon has it but in his case, I suspect, correctly,—and on occasion damned offensive. He was also—this is not hearsay—broody and sometimes depressed and, at such times, bloody rude.

In this connection I wish to call your attention to a story which was a great favourite with Leacock. It crops up again and again in his work, when he wants to illustrate what a joke is. It will certainly be known to most of you, but in this discussion I think it has a special meaning. The story goes that, perhaps a hundred and fifty years ago, a melancholy, depressed, lacklustre individual

143

presented himself in the consulting room of a great London physician, and asked for treatment for his immovable depression of spirits. The doctor examined him with care, and said at last, "My dear sir, there is nothing physically wrong with you, but you need cheering up. Now I suggest that you go to the theatre tonight and see the great clown, Grimaldi. He is funny beyond anything that you can imagine; he creates a whole world of amusement which will lift you quite out of yourself and leave you a better man. Come now, what do you say?" "Sir," replied the wretched patient, "*I* am Grimaldi."

Leacock loved that story. Many other humorists have loved it as well. They understand it better than other people.

Again and again in what he wrote about humour, Leacock stresses his belief that it should be kindly, that it should never wound, or call up any image which might give distress. He must have known that he was demanding the impossible, for humour is criticism of life, and criticism will always, at some time and in some quarter, beget resentment. The very fact of being a humorist is enough to set people against a man in certain circumstances. I recall to your minds the plight of P. G. Wodehouse, apparently the least offensive of humorists, and the darling of a million readers; yet, when he was in trouble—not really very serious trouble, as we now know—how the world turned on him! What he had done, or was supposed to have done, was made to seem twenty times worse because he was a humorist, a man who made his living by making a joke of life. Humour is not always innocent or kindly; it is a comment on life from a special point of view, and there will certainly be times when it will give sharp offence and be deeply resented—often to the astonishment of the humorist. But Leacock wanted, above all things, to be free from the charge of having wounded anyone. Was it because he was, deep within himself, aware of how deeply he might wound if he were not unfailingly vigilant?

The love of truth lies at the root of much humour. And at this point I beg leave to make a departure which may seem a curious one in a consideration of such a man as Leacock. There have been many books written about humour, which attempt to trace its sources, but none, I think, is so provocative of thought as *Wit and Its Relation to the Unconscious* by the late Sigmund

Freud. It is not an easy book to read, for it suffers greatly by translation into English, and it is apt to overwhelm us with that ennui which seems to be inseparable from writings which attempt to explain why things are funny—including Leacock's own. But it makes two points which are, I think, of great importance in any study of Leacock. The first is that humour is a way of saying things which would be intolerable if they were said directly. "Out of my great sorrows I make my little songs," said Heinrich Heine: the humorist might say, with equal truth, "Out of my great disenchantments I make my little jokes."

You have all, I suppose, read Leacock's wonderful little piece called *Boarding-House Geometry*? You recall that "A single room is that which has no parts and no magnitude"? That "the clothes of a boarding-house bed, though produced ever so far both ways, will not meet"? That "a landlady can be reduced to her lowest terms by a series of propositions"? Well, my friends, read what the author of that had to say about the seventeen Toronto boarding-houses in which he spent his student days in *The Boy I Left Behind Me* and then judge if Leacock has not said the intolerable in the only permissible way.

The second of Dr. Freud's conclusions which has a bearing on Leacock's humour is his assertion—backed by demonstration and proof of a kind too extended to be gone into here—that the object of the humorist is to strip away, momentarily, the heavy intellectual trappings of adult life, including so many things which we regard as virtues, and to set us free again in that happy condition which we enjoyed in the morning of life, when everything came to us freshly; when we did not have to make allowances for the limitations or misfortunes of others; when we did not have to be endlessly tender towards the feelings of others; when we dared to call a thing or a person stupid if they seemed stupid to us; when we lived gloriously from moment to moment, without thought for the past, or consideration for the future: when we were, indeed, as the lilies of the field. The humorist can restore us momentarily to that happy state. He pays a great price for his ability to do so, and our gratitude is by no means always forthcoming. But that is his special gift, and as the tragic writer rids us of what is petty and ignoble in our nature, the humorist rids us of much that is cautious, calculating and priggish. Both of

145

them permit us, in blessed moments of revelation, to soar above the common level of our lives. Judged by this demanding Freudian concept of humour, Stephen Butler Leacock emerges as a great humorist, for at his best he achieves the two desired ends—speaking truth, and setting us free from common concerns —and his humour rises from a mind itself comprehensive, vigorous and well-stored beyond the common measure.

We have already referred to that element in life which philosophers call *enantiodromia* or "the regulating function of opposites"—meaning simply that nothing exists without its direct contrary. If Leacock was so dogmatic on the point that humour must never hurt may it not be because he knew, deep within himself, that the truth in which so much humour is rooted can be extremely painful when it is brought to light? Certainly he knew that this could be true of other humorists than himself; read what he has written about W. S. Gilbert for confirmation of that. And as he wrote so much that was true of himself when he seemed to be writing about Dickens, I think that he wrote some of the truth about himself when he was writing about Gilbert. Leacock had one early and striking experience of the way in which humour can hurt when, in 1912, he published what is widely regarded as his finest book, *Sunshine Sketches of a Little Town*.

This book is a minor masterpiece, and of all his books it is the one most likely to live. It was quickly recognized as a work of importance, and it was hailed everywhere in the English-speaking world—everywhere, that is to say, except in the Little Town itself. There it gave deep and lasting offence.

I well remember the first time I mentioned the book to a former citizen of Orillia; it was about 1928 and I was an enthusiastic schoolboy in the school where Leacock himself had been a pupil. I shall not soon forget the outpouring of bitterness and wounded pride which I provoked in the lady to whom I spoke. The book, I was told, was an unforgivable piece of bad taste, in which the writer had pilloried good, kind people who had never done him any harm. Leacock was a nasty, sly, sneering man who made fun of people behind their backs. He was not a gentleman. And much more to the same effect.

Death settles all scores, and Orillia now publicizes itself, somewhat aggressively, as "The Sunshine Town." But while he lived,

Orillia never forgave Leacock. And he seems to have been very, very careful about giving offence in print again.

If we examine the book closely, we may see what the people of Orillia saw in it. It is a detailed portrait of an Ontario community which is not only extremely funny, but also ferocious and mordant. We are beguiled by the manner in which the book is written from giving too much attention to its matter. What it says, if we boil it down, is that the people of Mariposa were a self-important, gullible, only moderately honest collection of provincial folk; they cooked their election, they burned down a church to get the insurance, they exaggerated the most trivial incidents into magnificent feats of bravery; the sunshine in which the little town is bathed seems very often to be the glare of the clinician's lamp, and the author's pen is as sharp as the clinician's scalpel. There is love in the portrait, certainly, and indulgence for the folly of humankind. But what community has ever acclaimed a man because he showed it to be merely human? The deeper love in the book seems to be directed towards the writer's own youth, and it is made clear in the nostalgic chapters which begin and end the book that he has removed himself from Mariposa, and that any real, spiritual return is impossible, because the clock cannot be put back. We have, most of us, known Jeff Thorpe, and Judge Pepperleigh and his daughter, and Peter Pupkin, and Golgotha Gingham, and John Henry Bagshaw— but which of us would gladly admit that he was the original of one of these portraits? The humour is rooted in truth, but the truth is a very sharp knife when it is turned against our own breasts.

Leacock strove to make his humour kindly, after that. He never fully succeeded. The Old Adam which is deep in the heart of every real humorist could be heard chuckling from time to time.

Here again it would be impossible to refer to the comparison which was so often drawn, during his lifetime, between Leacock and Mark Twain. For the iron was in Mark Twain's soul, too, and there is a savagery in much of his fun which must startle any reader who has literary sensibility above the cabbage level.

But I do not see any resemblance between Leacock and Mark Twain which calls for special attention. As Leacock fell short of

Mark Twain's level in his total achievement and perhaps in the scope of his genius, so he far outsoared Mark Twain in the adult quality of his mind. Mark Twain wasted a great deal of time in attempting to apply the standards of a frontiersman to things which could not be judged in that way. Leacock's affectation of frontier attitudes and habits of speech was nothing more than the intellectual fancy dress of a highly educated, sophisticated and mature being.

I have not forgotten that, quite a long time ago, I set out to give you, briefly, the facts of Leacock's life. In 1900 he married Miss Beatrix Hamilton, of Toronto. She died in 1925 of cancer. He had one son, born in 1915. Leacock himself died of cancer in Toronto on March 28, 1944, in his 75th year. (Because I have talked so much about money, and stressed the important place which I believe it played in Leacock's development, it is relevant to say here that, although his McGill salary never exceeded $6,000 per annum, and although he spent freely, speculated heavily and gave open-handedly, he left about $140,000. Neither a large sum nor yet an inconsiderable one.)

Leacock's reputation is in decline at present, and inevitably so; such declines always follow the death of a literary man, and he is happy indeed if the beginning of the decline does not anticipate his last hour. But when this melancholy, apparently inevitable period is over, he will emerge as one who, living among us, fought the solitary fight of the literary artist in a special state of loneliness, for in spite of the vast audience which admired him and waited for his work, he was lonely. He lived at a time—a time which is still not completely past—when Canada was ready to acknowledge that a poet or a novelist might be an artist, worthy of the somewhat suspicious and controlled regard which our country accords to artists, but when a humorist was obviously a clown.

Yet we must beware of blaming Canada because Leacock did not follow the pattern which became clear with the publication of *Sunshine Sketches*, and develop into a great comic novelist. The intellectual climate of the country was not congenial to such development, certainly, but we must recognize that great artists create intellectual climates, and only artists of lesser rank are distorted or diminished by them. His failure to take that road which once seemed to lie so splendidly open before him was his own, and its causes lay within his own heart. Was it because the easier road lay in writing "funny pieces, just to laugh at"? Certainly that course brought big money, widespread popularity and was taxing only upon his powers of industry. The acclaim and the money helped to salve those early wounds inflicted by poverty and the sense of not being as good as the next fellow. If there was a failure to realize the highest that lay in his power— and I think there was—that may have been at the root of it.

Nevertheless, we are in danger, when we presume to rebuke the great dead for what they failed to do, of overlooking what they did do. And if we are to appreciate Leacock for what he was, forgetting all recollections of childhood readings of his work, and dismissing the popular legend of the genial professor from our minds, we must read his books afresh, with a new measure of adult understanding. Certainly let us not neglect the four chapters of autobiography, called *The Boy I Left Behind Me*, which must rank among the finest things he ever wrote and the finest things written by Canadians. Read the earlier Leacock in the light of those frank, heartfelt and somewhat bitter chapters, and new treasures will be revealed to you.

I have now carried the task which I outlined at the beginning as far as lies in my power. I promised nothing new—only a different and I hope, revealing, arrangement of what is already known. What emerges from it? A man of great spirit, deeply troubled; a literary artist, who fought his destiny; a man whose achievement, at its highest, puts him at the very top of any list of our Canadian writers. A great countryman of ours: a man to thank God for.

Lightning Source UK Ltd.
Milton Keynes UK
UKOW04f0631111017
310762UK00001B/17/P